HOW TO LIVE WITH KIDS AND ENJOY IT

BY IVERNA TOMPKINS
with Irene Harrell

Logos International
Plainfield, New Jersey

Also by Iverna Tompkins:
How to Be Happy in No Man's Land

To my two wonderful kids—

Contents

What Iverna Tompkins says about kids has a firm ring of truth. Mother of a son and a daughter, and counselor of other people's sons and daughters, she knows and loves kids, and they love her in return. Out of this mutual admiration society has come a rapport of real benefit to an understanding of the proper, God-ordained relationship between parents and their children.

Iverna's teaching is no systematic treatise, no sterile idealism. It deals with real kids as they are, and tackles the nitty-gritties in their lives with forthrightness. She's not been stuck away in some ivory tower of perfect parenthood with kids who cooperated with theoretical answers. She's dealt with a lot of the same kind of impossible situations most parents have faced, the yucky "there's no way out of this mess" deals. But God has shown her the way out, and has provided her with wisdom and answers because she's asked Him for help. In these pages she shares what she has learned.

Reading Iverna Tompkins' counsel won't make you put her on a pedestal of infallibility. You might even think she's wrong about some things. But you'll recognize that she "knows where it's at" and that she "has it all together" in a remarkable way. Her sharing with you is as friend to friend, not as authority to underling. But in a multitude of specific situations she dares to tell you what you can say, what you can do, if thus and such a thing happens at your house. The aim of all of this is to make you a better parent, better able to help your children enjoy their childhood and grow up to be happy, successful, contributing adult members of society, living up to the potential God has placed within them.

If there are trouble spots in your relationship with your children and you've had it up to here, or if things are pretty smooth but you'd like to be a better parent, *How to Live with Kids and Enjoy It* is for you.

I was brought up in a Christian home, according to scriptural principles, in the "nurture and admonition of the Lord." Then, at nineteen, I rebelled, left the church, and did my own thing for two years. During that time, I met a handsome marine, fell in love, and was married. Fourteen months later, while he was overseas, I realized that I was going to bear his child and that there was no way I could face the responsibility of bringing up a child unless I was living in a close relationship with God. So, like the prodigal, I returned to the Father's house and determined to live for the Lord the rest of my days.

When my husband came home, in place of the fun-loving party girl he had married, he found a sober, super-spiritual individual who was taking motherhood very seriously. She didn't waste any time, but sat him down right away and announced in no uncertain terms that things were going to be different in her home from that point on. No beer in the refrigerator, the cigarettes would have to go. . . .

Ministers and church members patted me on the back. "You're doing the right thing, Iverna," they told me. "Just take your stand, and God will honor you for it."

No one suggested to me that maybe there was some reasonable, God-honoring way in which I might bring up our children in a way that was pleasing to God without depriving them of a father by my rigidly legalistic attitude about everything.

Twelve rocky years later, the inevitable happened. My home broke up. My husband left me for someone he could live with.

When I began to complain to the Lord and to ask why He had let such a terrible thing happen, He showed me that He isn't a God who will back any stand just because I happen to take it. He is honor bound to honor only His own Word—

which was far removed from the legalistic approach I had taken and attempted to enforce on my husband. I had missed the whole spirit of the law, which is love, in my insistence on keeping strictly to the letter of it. "The letter killeth," the Bible says, and I had found it out—the hard way. What I learned through the failure of my marriage made me examine carefully the whole business of human relationships, particularly the matter of parent-child relationships. Having failed as a wife, I did not want to fail as a mother. I did not want to make any mistakes with my children if I could help it.

One important thing I saw at the outset was that I could not *tell* my children one thing and expect them to believe it if at the same time I was inadvertently teaching them the exact opposite. I could not, for instance, expect them to believe me when I *told* them God is love if my life indicated that He was a big cop up in the sky, watching their every move. The only way I could teach them that God is love was by showing them that love myself, in how I lived before them.

Living with kids in a relationship that reflects the love of God isn't something that just comes naturally. If it were, Paul would never had written to Titus that the older women were to *teach* the younger women to love their children (Titus 2:4). Loving our children is something that has to be worked at—intelligently, prayerfully, consistently— because loving is not mushy sentimentality. Real parental loving has many facets. It can be very tough, but its ultimate aim will always be to equip our youngsters for mature, responsible, happy adulthood of their own. Real loving strives toward obedience to the Scripture that admonishes parents, "Train up a child in the way he should go . . ." (Prov. 22:6).

I have found that understanding our kids—and helping

them to understand us instead of just to bow to us as authority figures—are two important keys to successful parenthood. In these pages, I have attempted to set down some experiences with my own children, and some experiences of other parents with their children, which have helped me understand kids. It is my prayer that this sharing might help you toward more wonderfully fulfilling parenthood, toward a richer, fuller life with and for *your* kids.

1

What Makes 'Em Tick?

Heaving kind of a tired sigh, I finished my work log, tucked it in my desk drawer, and rummaged in my purse for the car keys. It had been a hard day, and I was weary, but there was a tingle of excitement in me as I put on my coat and headed for the parking lot.

My good neighbor, Barbara, took care of my children for me while I worked as a probation officer to earn a living for my family. She always had the kids ready and waiting for my return at the end of the day. I could hardly wait to swoop two-year-old Danny up in my arms and prop him on one hip while I hugged seven-year-old Debbie to me on the other side.

Stopping for a red light, I caught a glimpse of myself in the mirror on my sun visor. I was grinning a mile wide, just at the thought of my children. I wondered if other parents felt the same way about theirs.

Turning the corner onto my block, I craned my neck for a glimpse of Debbie and Danny.

They were nowhere in sight! But they were always out waiting unless it was raining. What could be wrong?

I hurried out of the car and into Barbara's house. The center of attraction was a large cardboard box in the middle of the floor. Debbie and Danny were on their knees peering intently inside the box at a mother cat and five wiggly, mewing, newborn kittens, their tiny tails poking straight up in the air.

For a moment, I was jealous at being upstaged by mere kittens, but then I was on my knees with the children, ooohing and aaahing over the fuzzy miracles of new life.

After we went home, we talked about the new kittens while I got supper on the table. Then the three of us went to church where I was serving as organist for the choir. Later that night, after I'd heard the children's prayers and tucked them into bed, I thought about the whole business of parenthood for divorcees like me and for parents in more ideal family situations.

The episode with the kittens had brought into sharp focus for me two of the prime requisites of successful parenthood: a willingness to share with children in what is important to them, and an openness to understand and cooperate with what makes them tick.

It's years later, now, and I'm no longer a counselor in a probation office or a church organist, but I've not forgotten what I learned then. Today, Debbie is happily married to a young man who is studying for the ministry, and Danny is six-feet-one and in his last year of high school. During their growing-up years, my kids taught me a lot. Living with them and counseling other people's children, I learned to look behind kids' outward behavior to see what was really going on inside them. For instance:

A three-year-old was trying to put a lid on a jar, and he was turning it the wrong way. Mother came along and said, "Here, honey, let me show you how. You should turn it *this* way—"

The child shouted, "No!" and tried to jerk the jar from her hand. The jar crashed to the floor, mom snatched the child up, spanked him soundly, and put him to bed. Then, still seething, she swept up the broken glass.

A five-year-old boy wanted to try fishing with an empty fishhook. When his father noticed what was happening, he pulled the hook out of the water, put a worm on it, and threw it back. A few minutes later, the child caught a whopper. He didn't seem especially pleased about it, though, and when he thought his father wasn't looking, he kicked the fish off the edge of the pier and back into the water. You *know* what the father did when he caught a glimpse of the action out of the corner of his eye.

Another child polished his own shoes. The shoes looked pretty awful, but the child beamed, proud of what he had done. Then mom came along and touched up the imperfectly polished shoes for him. Later, she wandered why she caught him deliberately scuffing his toes along in the dirt.

In each of the three cases above, we have what looks like rebellion in the child, but it's not that simple. In the midst of what looks like a negative, rebellious reaction, the child is actually making a forcefully positive statement:

"I'm me. I want to live by my own ideas. I *need* to do my own thing. I have to express my own will once in a while."

When parents feel they are supposed to break a child's

will instead of to encourage its expression in acceptable ways, the effort frustrates everybody. Actually, a child's will is not made to be broken, it is made to be directed into the right channels. Parents live longer, and enjoy life more, when they see this and encourage independence and individuality in their children instead of trying to fit them into molds of conformity. Children can learn something important by turning a jar lid the wrong way, by fishing with an empty fishhook, and by polishing their own shoes, however imperfectly.

Some time ago, I read about a little boy who had gone to a restaurant to eat with his family. The waitress was unusually perceptive, and when she was taking the orders, she began with the child. She seemed not to hear what other people were saying he *could* have, she just asked him what he wanted, and when he told her, she wrote it down.

Well, being asked to give his own order in a restaurant was such a new thing for this child, he could hardly get over the feeling of worth and recognition it gave him. After the meal, he got his mother's attention long enough to tell her what the experience had done for him. Still starry-eyed with wonderment, he said, "Mom, you know that waitress in the restaurant? She thought I was *real!*"

Children *are* real. They need to be confident of our awareness of their reality. We can profit by affirming our children at every opportunity.

Suppose our child shouts, "Mommy, there's a dragon in the front yard!" We could look out the window and lecture, "There's no dragon out there. You mustn't tell things that aren't so."

Or we could look out the window and see that dragon for ourselves, throw our hand up protectively around our throat, and holler a little.

"Oh, mercy! Look how he's breathing fire on the shrubbery! What do you think we should do? Call the zoo—the
fire department—the police—or what?"

Maybe the child will tell us he thinks it's a friendly dragon.
Maybe he'll want to go for a ride on his back. We could try to
talk him out of it—or we could go outside and help him
climb on. Show him how to grip the saddlehorn, and make
sure you get his feet in the stirrups so he won't fall off. Put
the imaginary reins in his hands and go back into the house.
When he comes in to tell you where he's been and what he's
seen, you can express your wonder and delight at that, too.

A child won't become a sociopath or a liar from this kind
of fun. He'll have a fertile imagination, an active mind. Our
great inventors, our creative geniuses, didn't come from
kids who were never encouraged to let their minds roam. A
creative imagination is to be encouraged, not squelched, in
a youngster, and so is a healthy curiosity.

Several years ago, an eight-year-old in our church said to
her mother, "I've simply got to have a counseling session
with Iverna."

"Well, honey," her mother said, "you can't have a counseling session with Iverna right now. She's not scheduling any
counseling sessions this week while the pastor's gone."

"But I've got to ask her a question," the little girl per-
sisted, deadly serious.

"I felt very inadequate," the mother told me later, "but I
asked her if maybe I could answer the question for her."

The little girl studied her mother's face for a moment, as
if she was trying to decide whether or not her mother could
be trusted with such a weighty matter, and finally she said,
"Well, I needed to ask Iverna if dinosaurs were here before
Jesus or after."

Of course, the child's real question had nothing to do with

prehistoric animals. The youngster was really wanting to say, "I have a mind; I think, and I'd like for some grownups to be aware of the fact."

The mother wisely took advantage of the opportunity to interact intellectually with her youngster. They looked up "dinosaurs" in the encyclopedia and learned some things together.

When my Debbie was four years old, she and a little boyfriend about her age were sitting out on the curb, talking earnestly together about something. The little boy's mother and I wondered what could be gripping their attention, and so we sneaked up behind them to eavesdrop on the conversation.

"Well, do you really believe the bad people will burn up in hell?" one asked the other.

"Yeah, I do."

"And will they keep on burning up forever?"

"Yep. Forever and forever—"

My friend and I were amazed at the "theological" content of our children's conversation and realized that we had been underestimating their intellectual abilities.

Kids thrive on intellectual stimulation, whether they're toddlers or teens. Whatever their ages, we can welcome their questions. When we don't know the answers, we can go to the library together and look them up.

In looking at what makes kids tick, we find their active minds in extra-active bodies. Most kids seem to enjoy activities that give them physical pleasure and satisfaction. They love to swing, play baseball, skip down the sidewalk, go swimming, wiggle in their seats at school. They are zestful adventurers, always on the go.

Sometimes parents don't realize that it is necessary for

children to express their youthful energies in an abundance of physical activity. We might feel our youngsters are deliberately crowding us to the limit, pushing, pushing, all the time. Youngsters sense this, and instead of deterring them, it seems to egg them on. It's uncanny that they seem to know just how far they can go with it.

"Oh, boy! My mom was just about ready to blow up—"

Kids can seem like set mousetraps, just waiting to spring when we're least suspecting. It's one of their more successful ways of getting attention. We can enjoy it, too, by joining in the game once we're onto what they're up to.

A positive acceptance of children's normal physical and mental activity levels helps us to enjoy our kids— independence, imagination, curiosity, physical exuberances, and all. According to God's written Word, children are *meant* to be enjoyed: "Children are a gift from God; they are his reward. Children born to a young man are like sharp arrows to defend him. Happy is the man who has his quiver full of them" (Ps. 127:3-5a TLB).

2

Listening—the Key to Understanding Your Kids

"Mom, you don't listen to me any more!" Danny accused me one day.

Me, not listen? I'd always prided myself on the fact that I *did* listen. Why, I had considered myself the best listening mother in the world. But with Danny's accusation came a startling realization that what he said was true. I couldn't have been really listening, because I had just asked him if the girl he was dating was a Christian. Some corner of my memory told me that I'd asked him the same question before, about the same girl. If I had been *really* listening, I'd have remembered that I had asked the question before, and I'd have remembered his answer, too.

Real listening involves an investment of ourselves far beyond merely making polite conversation. Real listening is in-depth identification with the child and a serious attempt to understand his point of view.

One day I was hollering at Danny for not scouring out his bathtub. We had had words on the same subject in the past, but the conflict had never been resolved.

"Mom," he asked me, patiently controlling his exaspera-tion at my tirade, "why is it so important for me to scour my tub every day? Nobody uses it but me, and the tub doesn't look *so* terrible if I miss cleaning it for a whole week. Be-sides, I'm the only one who sees it, unless you happen to poke your head in just to check up on me. Who cares how it looks?"

Well, Dan got through to me that day, because I was really listening, involving myself in his point of view. I had to admit it *shouldn't* actually matter all that much whether or not his tub was sparkling like a cleanser commercial, but it *did* matter to me.

We should have been able to settle on a compromise. Dan might have promised to scour his tub once a week without being reminded, unless it got really grimy-looking even to him. If that happened, he'd scrub it more often. In the meantime, I could have promised not to bug him about it. We could both have heaved a sigh of relief that an awful area of conflict had been ended. But it didn't happen that way, because some area of pride in me still insisted that the tub be sparkling all the time, not just once a week. I didn't change my rule, he didn't change his attitude, but we un-derstood each other, because we had both listened. That helped.

Other parents tell me the same thing happens in their parent-child relationships. The parent acknowledges the relative reasonableness of a child's attitude about some-thing, but still insists it be done his way. There's no harm done as long as the channels of communication are kept open. We don't have to agree about everything in order to love one another. We can disagree—without being disagreeable about it. But we do have to listen.

Parents of outgoing, independent-thinking youngsters are often presented with persuasive arguments as they listen. My son can argue so logically that sometimes I reel in my own principles for a minute.

"Look at it this way, mom," he'll say. Then he'll present a case for his side that would sway the most able jury in the land. I almost always see his point, but God is merciful, and I see the real point, too. Sometimes I stick to my guns. Sometimes I change my mind. The communication between us is a good thing, from his point of view and mine, no matter what the outcome. When we really listen, we can't really lose.

Real listening is vital because there's no way we can know another person or understand his point of view without hearing him.

Suppose my child wants to have a dog. If I don't listen to his reasons, my answer may be a flat no. I might explain my decision:

"You're involved in so much at school these days, you wouldn't have time to take the dog for his daily walk. I'd be left having to walk him, feed him, take him to the vet for shots, and all that. I just don't have time for a dog." That would be that.

But what if I listened first to his reasons for wanting a dog?

"Mom, when you're gone, I get lonesome in the apartment with nobody to play with. I don't have any friends here. But if I had a dog—"

Identifying with his point of view, I might make an

affirmative decision after all and head for the pet shop. Since a pet would mean so much to my child, I might consider it a good investment of my time to walk the dog once in a while, and to do other things for him. By listening, I learn the real needs of my children and am put in a frame of mind where I am willing to meet those needs.

The kind of listening required of parents is not judgmental listening.

My child might come into the house in tears, sniffling, "Janie hit me." Times without number, my first reaction has been a negative, "What did you do to her?"

It would have been far better to say, "How did it happen?" and not put my child on the defensive. Such an impartial response could encourage a healing outpouring, instead of closing a damper of frustration on the cause of the trouble.

When we don't listen, we're limited to our own perspective, which may be a very one-sided thing. Besides that, our refusal to listen to our children teaches them not to listen to us. A mass of misunderstandings is the inevitable result.

True listening is not the same thing as tolerating a period of verbiage. Neither is it merely letting the child say his piece so that when he is finished we can tell him what we'd already decided. Real listening has to include a willingness to change our minds and a willingness to consider a compromise.

I used to be quite annoyed over the clutter of candy wrappers, tennis shoes, stationery, pop cans and comic books that accumulated under Dan's bed.

"But, mom," he used to protest when I'd say something about it, "I always clean those things up in a day or two. It doesn't make sense for me to have to get out of bed to carry a pop can to the kitchen when I'm reading at night or to put my tennis shoes in the closet when I'm going to put them on again the first thing in the morning."

What he said sounded reasonable enough, but I couldn't back down all the way, and I told him so. I don't remember which of us thought of a workable compromise, but one day we got a sturdy cardboard box and cut the sides down so it could slide under his bed. He began to keep all his under-bed paraphernalia there, handy for him to reach, yet quickly slid out of the way when we wanted to sweep or dust the floor. I was satisfied because everything was in the box, and Dan was happy with the arrangement, too.

The compromise couldn't have happened if we hadn't been able to listen and really *hear* each other's point of view.

Many teenagers feel, with rich justification, that there's no future in saying anything to their parents, because parents never listen.

"What's the use of talking to my folks?" kids have asked me many times. "They never listen—they never change their minds no matter what I say." Too often, that's true.

A child may say to a counselor, "I just don't have any freedom. My parents are too strict. They never let me go anywhere with the other kids."

When parents hear this, they are likely to sputter, "But that isn't so at all. Johnny belongs to this and that, and he goes here and there, and every once in a while, we let him go to another place—"

As long as we are occupied with defending our own actions, we are not listening. We are not trying to understand our youngster. We have to learn to deal with the situation as our child sees it, not with the situation as we think he ought to see it.

Not long ago, a youngster told me, "My parents don't love me." When I conveyed that to her parents, they protested,

"But that's not *true!* We *do* love our child."

Whether we love our child or not, if our child thinks we don't, then that unlove is true for him, at least for the moment, and something needs to be done to reassure him.

"But how can I do this all-important listening to *my* child?" parents have asked me. "Johnny is so quiet—he hardly ever has anything to say to me."

If you have a child who is a real introvert, and you want to bring him out of his shell, check your memory to see if he's been an introvert all his life or if he's fallen into it recently. Introverted teenagers are generally kids who have not learned to give of themselves. The only way some people can learn to give of themselves is to have it demanded of them.

With our teenager, we can begin by letting him know that we need him for something. We can ask his opinions about things, without using questions he can turn off with yes or no answers. We can involve him in discussions, asking, "What do you think about the national political situation?" If he says he doesn't know, we can acknowledge that of course no one *knows,* but we'd just like to hear what he thinks about it. We may be amazed at the depth of his response when he thinks we're really interested.

There's an art to keeping conversation coming from our children instead of always telling them what's what. When they become comfortable with talking to us, they will begin to respond to others as well. It will be a progressive thing if we'll get it started and give them some practice.

In the midst of doing this, we need to keep in mind the purpose of the conversation. It's not that our children might impart accurate, scientifically verifiable information, but that they might be open in sharing with us. For that reason, it would be wrong to correct them if they misquote a statistic, mispronounce a word, or draw some illogical conclusion, embellishing it with knowledge they don't have. We must keep in mind that we're not working on their intellectual content, we're working on their ability to converse in a meaningful way. There will be other opportunities to correct any misinformation without squelching the flow of communication.

Every listening parent knows that nothing is off-limits for discussion as far as a child is concerned. Things adults might discuss in veiled terms, if at all, a youngster feels free to blurt right out at the least opportune moment.

"Mom, I can't stand to talk to Mrs. So-and-So. Her breath stinks."

It's easy for us to react to such embarrassing outbursts with a careful, "Shhh! It's not nice to talk about such things." But it is better for us to seize every opportunity to teach our child something he needs to know. Instead of just shushing the child, we can tell him, "That's why we use mouthwash, so our breath won't offend anybody."

A surprising number of teenagers have never been taught by their parents to use an underarm deodorant, and somehow the TV commercials haven't sunk in either. Girls might get some instruction about such things in gym class, but boys may not.

A teenage girl spoke to me one day about a very fine Christian young man.

"He's just perfect in every other way," she said, "but I can't stand to be around him because he has such strong body odor. What can I do about it?"

There wasn't much she *could* do, without dying of embarrassment. Fortunately, a church counselor took it upon himself to go to the boy and tell him why he should use an underarm deodorant. The boy received the advice graciously, in spite of his embarrassment. The last I heard, romance had flourished, wedding bells had rung, the union had been blessed with beautiful children, and the whole family used deodorant.

Admittedly, we all have other things to do than just to listen to our youngsters and respond to what they are telling us. But we can try to give them our undivided attention for a few minutes—however long they need—before they leave home in the morning and the first time we're together after that.

We need to know the frustrations of the night, the problems of yesterday, even though they're past. Sometimes kids need to make a confession, express a change of attitude, or confess their fear of going back to school. They need to unload all this to somebody, and it's better for them to talk to us than to some kid at the bus stop. The hearer needs to be the one who can give guidance.

When you've been out and come back home, don't glance at the headlines first, shuffle through the mail, or go up to change your clothes. First, give yourself to your kids, let them get off their chests whatever they need to. Learn to read them. When you're paying *real* attention, you'll pick up the import of what they *don't* say, as well as what they do say.

Those of us who are working mothers can't consider ourselves off duty when we leave the office at five o'clock. We remain on duty, but in a different role.

The kids have probably been living for the moment when we come in from work. They want to tell us everything that has happened to them.

If we come home with an attitude that says, "I've got to get dinner on the table so I can get that over with, and then I can relax," we defeat the whole evening with our kids. But if we go in and invite our kids to pour out to us whatever they need to, we avoid a lot of unnecessary frustration for them and for ourselves.

After dinner is over, the dishes are done, and kids' immediate needs have been met, mom can have some time for herself. It's good for children to recognize that mothers are persons, too, with needs of their own.

Mom doesn't say to the kids, "Okay, your time is up. Shove off. Now it's my time for me." She gets it across in more subtle ways, saying, perhaps, "I'm going to take my shower now, honey."

If she's been really available to them up to that time, they'll be happy and accepting, not clamoring for more because they've been shortchanged to begin with.

When we try to avoid the extra two hours of "duty," we find ourselves feeling so guilty we don't enjoy any of the time we've kept for ourselves. And the kids don't leave us alone either.

If we have a good rapport with our youngster, occasionally we can afford to say, "Honey, I'm busy right now. I can stop what I'm doing so we can talk, or we can talk in about an hour when I'll be finished with all this. Which would you like?"

When the rapport is there, and we've treated our child in a trustworthy manner in the past, not letting him down when we'd promised something, he'll know he can count on us, and his decision will be an honest one.

But if that rapport hasn't been firmly established, and he comes out with something like, "Oh, it really doesn't matter, mom. I don't have to talk to you about it," then we'd be well advised to stop whatever we're doing and let him know that he is more important to us than anything else. Meeting our children's need to be heard, giving them the assurance and security of our attention and love should always have the highest priority in our schedule.

This is a busy world. We're busy people. Even women who are not working outside the home have so much to do that they make schedules for themselves. By nine o'clock in the morning, they have an idea of what their day is going to include. We live a scheduled life—or we get run over. But schedules are made to be broken when our youngsters need us. We need to listen to them—even if we have to leave the rug half vacuumed, or if dinner will be an hour late— because it's an eternal life we're dealing with.

A simple, "What are you doing, mom?" should often be translated, "I need some attention from you, mom." If we can't involve our child in what we're doing, we can quit it. If two minutes of our undivided attention is all our kid requires, wonderful. If it's twenty minutes, that's wonderful, too. But we let him judge the time according to his needs. We don't try to hurry him off. We only defeat our own purpose that way.

If we don't always have lots of time with our youngsters, it's doubly important that the time we do spend with them is unsparingly theirs.

The quantity of spoken conversation is never the criterion of real listening. Father and son can sit side by side for hours not talking, and know they've been together. On the other hand, they can talk a mile a minute without really meeting minds if either of them is preoccupied with something else. Real listening is paying attention to the other person—whether or not any words are spoken. Real listening is the stuff of which family togetherness is made.

3

Your Kids and You

Some years ago, a young mother of my acquaintance was more than a little frustrated with raising her four kids. They were growing as fast as dandelions, and she told me, "Sometimes I wish I could just take them to your house and leave them. You could bring them up for me, and I could just rest."

"Betty," I said, "I want to tell you something. For your own four kids, you're undoubtedly the best mother in the whole wide world."

It's almost always true, that for your youngster, you're the best parent in the world, because that child has an emotional attachment for you. He has identified himself with you.

It's not difficult for adults to make identification with

19

kids. I can love all kinds of kids and they know it. I could walk in, pick up a strange child, take it into my home, and in an hour, I'd feel that it was my own flesh and blood. But that doesn't mean that the child would make the same kind of identification with me. After a while, it would cry for whoever means mamma to him. "Mamma" might be the natural mother, a foster parent, an adoptive parent, or the maid who had taken care of it as long as it could remember. Once this "mamma" or "daddy" identification has been made, it cannot be broken without some damage or hurt to the youngster.

In wartime, fathers are taken away. Suddenly, daddy is gone. Mothers can understand and grow to accept this, but it's far more difficult for children.

"Someone took my daddy," doesn't mean the same thing as, "Someone took my husband, the man I love." What it means to the youngster is, "Someone tore off my arm—a part of me is gone."

Psychiatrists find a tie-in between such emotional traumas as the absence of a parent and such physical ailments as constipation. A child might be thinking, "I got hurt when someone took something away from me, and so I'm going to hold on to everything else that's mine—forever."

It is impossible to overestimate the importance of a parent in a child's life. A child is secure when he feels his parents are adequate to meet his needs. Confidence in their adequacy is vital to his sense of well-being.

There are two reasons why parents, alone or together, seldom communicate the vital assurance of their adequacy to their children. In the first place, they feel inadequate. They are afraid to reassure their youngsters, because they feel that they can't carry through. In the second place, there is, particularly in Christians, a false humility. They think it would be sinful pride to say, "I can do all things for you." And so they say to their youngsters, "Well, mother can't do it, so we'll just ask Jesus to do it for us."

This is beautiful—but ridiculous. What it says to children is, "The thing that you can see, this tangible me, will not be enough for you, but something very intangible, way up there beyond your understanding or comprehension, *that* will meet all your needs."

How should mothers who depend on the Lord Jesus Christ handle this? We can tell our kids, truthfully, "I get my guidance from Jesus. He gives me the answers. He gives me my strength, and I'm your strength." That gives them confidence, because they can *see* us.

"We've got mom," they can say. And we don't have to be afraid that we will become an idol in place of God to them. Moms and dads fall from their pedestals soon enough, but there is a time when our kids *need* to idolize us, *need* to think we're the greatest things on wheels, the strongest persons in the world.

When my little boy was about four years old, he brought a little playmate home with him one day. The playmate was about a head higher than my kid, and he stood with his arms folded, looking up at me with a fierceness that *had* to be hereditary.

Danny said, "Mom, *can't* you lick his dad?"

I took a deep breath, remembered seeing the kid's absolute giant of a father out mowing his lawn one day, and lied my heart out.

"Oh, I suppose I could," I said.

It was not a time to let my kid down. It was a time to keep him sure that I was superwoman. And I didn't have to worry about climbing down off my pedestal some day. When Danny got to be ten, he knew I couldn't lick anybody.

He thought I was the weakest woman in the world.

"Wait, mom, I'll do it for you," is what he said at that age. He opened all the jars for me, moved all the furniture, and replaced all the burned-out light bulbs, because he knew I was a weakling. Kids just naturally outgrow their idolizing of parents; we don't have to guard against it. We can enjoy it while it's there.

A child comes home from school, sticks his head in the door, and calls out, "Mom!"

"Yes, I'm right here in the kitchen," she answers. The child may go on out to play without even looking in the kitchen. He may not come in until suppertime, but he knows mom is there—and that's what he needed to know. If mom didn't answer when he called, he would probably go all through the house looking for her, thinking his whole day was ruined because she was out of place. Sometimes his simple cry of "Mom!" doesn't say, "I need to talk to you now." It says, "I need to know you're here, just in case I need you. I have to have that confidence in my life. I require the stability you provide."

One mother reported that her second grader came flying in from school, grabbed an apple, gave her mother a peck on the cheek, and then went outside to play with the neighborhood kids. A little later, she flew back inside again for a drink of water. She took time to say, "Mom, if I didn't have you I'd be awful lonesome," and dashed back out to rejoin the games. What the child said was true—her security was in her mother, not in the gang.

One night my son was running around in the parking lot of the church while I was inside conducting choir practice. He skidded and fell, cutting his knee wide open. Someone called me, and I ran out and cleaned the cut and talked to him a little while. It was obvious that the cut would need stitches in order to heal properly.

"Danny," I asked him, "would you like for me to take you to the clinic now, do you want someone else to take you now, or would you like to wait until choir practice is over and we can go together? Which would suit you best?"

"It's okay with me to wait until after choir practice, mom," he assured me. "It really doesn't hurt too bad."

I took his word for it and went back inside to help with the music making. Afterward, I took him to the doctor's office. Danny didn't have to test me by putting himself first, because he could see that I was doing that already. Besides, he had four or five little kids waiting with him, all of them duly impressed by all the blood and by how brave he was not to cry.

The relationship of parent to child has an overwhelming influence on the child, for good or for bad. When youngsters don't have good relationships with their parents, sometimes they seek to find such relationships in marriage.

A young teenage girl might feel attracted toward an older man because she needs a father. She doesn't realize the nature of the attraction, thinks it's love, and they get married and live miserably ever after.

Sometimes it works the other way. A little girl who is a born mother discards her dollies, makes herself up to look older than she is, and attracts a teenage boy who doesn't have a good relationship with his mother. They get married, and she takes on a misguided mother role, telling him where to go and what to do. The whole relationship is contrary to God's order from the beginning, and there's no chance for happiness unless something changes drastically.

Many of the too-young marriages of today have come about because parents have failed to understand that God has given them the ability—as well as the responsibility—to meet all kinds of needs in their youngsters.

The moment a child is born or adopted into our home, it's as if we have taken an oath before God, saying, "I assume total responsibility for preparing this child for adulthood." In one church I served, parents bringing infants for dedication were asked, "Do you, under God, in the presence of these witnesses, hereby state that you will do everything possible to live the life of Christ before them, and as early as possible lead them into an understanding of their personal acceptance of Jesus Christ as Savior?" When we received an affirmative answer to that, we presented the child to the Lord, asking for His protection, health, and guidance throughout life.

The kind of life we live before our children has a lot to do with how they turn out. This is true because of the nature of the identification children make with their parents. This identification develops over a period of time, but little girls feel like their mothers, and boys feel like their fathers by the time they're sixteen, at least. Being better than mother or better than father causes guilt in their minds or in their consciences.

"I shouldn't have anything better than my mother had," a girl might say to herself, and if she has an alcoholic father, she might marry an alcoholic.

"I shouldn't have a better wife than my father has," a boy might reason, and he will marry what he saw in his mother—a lousy housekeeper, a sloppy dresser, a woman careless about everything.

Sometimes we find a child from a drinking family who is so against liquor that you couldn't pour it down him. But that's not always the case. Many kids follow in their father's—or mother's—staggering footsteps, right into the gutter.

This awareness that they might turn out like their parents scares them. The greatest fear in my daughter's young life was that someday she'd be as loudmouthed as her mother. She used to say that she just hated women preachers. Subconsciously, she was afraid that she might turn out to be one. (She didn't, but her husband is studying for the ministry.)

It is natural for your children to be proud of the good things in your life and frightened about your negatives, because they feel they might be like you. We can help them understand that while it is a natural thing for them to follow the leader, they are also individuals in their own right, not merely extensions of us.

"Debbie," I told my daughter one day when she seemed concerned about these things, "God won't make you just like me. He's going to make you just like Jesus."

Parents don't usually say that, because it's kind of an ego-builder to them when their kids say, "I'm going to be just like my dad." We need to encourage kids to believe that they can beat us a mile if they want to. In their struggle for independence from what we are, they may pull far away from our apron strings and do things we'd never dream of doing, just to prove to themselves, "I'm not like my dad. I'm not like my mom. They're holy, and see me? I'm worldly."

We can prevent some of this. We can reassure them explicitly, "Son, in some things, I can see you're like me; in some things, I can see you're like your father; but in other things, you're unique—not like either one of us, but just yourself."

If we're going to tell them they're like anyone, we can use

it positively, praising them for some good quality—patience, love, generosity, athletic skill. We should never use, "You're just like so and so," in a condemning way. Chances are, we'd want to retract such a statement later, saying, "Oh, honey, I'm *so* sorry. I shouldn't have said that. I didn't mean it," but there'd be no way to take the words back. They'd be indelibly imprinted on our youngster's mind, and he'd think he could never change.

Girls in trouble have told me that they had warred for years not to be like their mother, but they turned out like her anyway. They couldn't help themselves.

Where did they get that concept? They grew up with it. Every time dad was mad at them, he yelled, "You're just like your mother!" Finally, the kids believed it and it happened. Understanding these things, we can guard against them.

Some fathers are afraid to try to raise children. In part, this is because they cannot accept rejection in the same way that most mothers can. It's an inborn thing. When a man moves out to a youngster, makes some overture of friendship, and the youngster rejects him in any degree, the male ego is crushed. As a result, the father is afraid to venture forth again for fear the same rebuff might occur. This can go on for years. A father can live in the same house with his children and yet be totally apart from them, just because he's afraid of rejection.

Many women don't realize this. They think that innate paternal love is just like maternal love, but it's not. A man can get so angry with his offspring that he will break all emotional ties and cut them off completely. But most mothers cannot do that. A mother can get raging mad at her child—he can hurt her and crush her and do desecration to her name—and still she is able to throw her arms open and say, "Honey, I love you."

Mothers are like that. They can't help it. The forgiving love of a mother is part of God's provision for the preservation of the species.

There are some fathers, of course, who can let their parental feelings show, who are free to let parental love come forth. These are the fathers who play with the baby, who take the kid to the store whenever they go, who wouldn't go hunting or fishing without inviting an older child to go along.

When you find a home that has both maternal love and paternal love in full expression, you find a beautiful thing. But when either of these ingredients is missing, someone must endeavor to compensate, to make up the lack, in order to create the atmosphere of love and security.

When paternal love is insecure and a youngster appears to reject father, mother can step into the breach and rescue the situation.

A father might say to his teenage daughter, "Would you like to go with me to the seed store? I want to plant some grass this afternoon."

It takes him twenty minutes to get up the nerve to ask her, because he's so afraid she might say no. His fears are realized when she contemplates the boring business of visiting a dusty, hot seed store and turns her father down with a flat, "No, I don't want to go."

Mother, seeing that father is about to disintegrate, can step in and say (quietly, so only Mary can hear), "Honey, he *wants* you to go with him."

Mary calls out, "Wait for me, dad. I've changed my mind. I'll be there in a minute." Suddenly, everything's all right again.

Mary wasn't rejecting her father, but his ego would react as if she were. That's why it is helpful for the mother to get the child to consider the *relationship* reason for going—to be with her daddy. Considering that, she naturally wants to go.

Many fathers don't know what to do with their teenage daughters. They don't know how to be with them in a way that is beneficial to the growing youngster. Some girls don't mow the lawn, some don't like to go fishing, aren't interested in sports, don't know what goes on under the hood of the car, and father is left not knowing what to talk about. Often father ignores the teenage daughter until she gets married and furnishes him with some grandchildren to whom he can relate.

Because teenage girls need a strong relationship with their father, mothers should come to the rescue in every helpful way they can. When father and daughter have come back from the store with grass seed and weed killer, mother can ask the daughter to help father in the yard. Doing things together can often serve the same purpose as talking things over. Maybe father and daughter will get acquainted in the process. Stranger things have happened. And when they have become acquainted, mother won't have to be flinging the life preserver so often. Daughter will automatically respond to her dad's need for her company. He, in turn, will feel sufficiently secure with her that he won't interpret reluctance to go to the feed store as a rejection of himself.

Daughters need their dads during the teen years probably more than at any other time. And yet, this is the age when many seem to reject their dads altogether.

One father told me, "Honestly, I've reached out to my daughter every way I know how, but she always rejects me. There's a wall there that I can't seem to get through."

This is characteristic of the oedipal stage, the time when subconsciously every girl relates to her daddy as the love of her life. That's why she's so shy and rejecting at times, and so very loving at other times. It takes a few years for her to get all these things sorted out in her mind. In the meantime, she's vacillating, and the father doesn't know how to handle her.

More fathers than you might realize get sexually involved with their youngsters during this period in their lives. They don't know how to cope with a passionate young girl caught up in drives she herself doesn't understand. Trouble is a natural result. As soon as it happens, the daughter points a finger of shame. Mother gets mad, the court gets mad, and father gets the ax. Everybody shakes his head and clucks, "Isn't that terrible? He must be sick. I can't imagine such a thing."

Maybe you can't imagine it either, but it happens. It *is* horrible, but it's natural. The possibility of improper sexual overtones can be completely overcome, however, by frequent physical expression of the right kind of wholesome emotional warmth. We can make it a habit to maintain physical contact with our teen—a firm hug or even a back rub now and then. Father/daughter and mother/son relationships are areas where a good heterosexual transfer can be made. If daughter learns to trust dad and his affection, then it's easier for her to reach out to other males in a right relationship, not expecting the worst from them. It is terribly important that fathers convey to their daughters a feeling of warmth and safety where men are concerned.

Mothers are sometimes aware of a real inner conflict and turmoil when husbands require attention at the same time the children do. A little advance planning can help to eliminate problems in this area. We can begin with a priority list that takes into account our own special family circumstances. If the husband is at home very little, being with

him should be at the very top of our priority list when he is
around.

Mothers can arrange to take care of most of the needs of
the older children when their husbands are not at home.
Then they won't feel neglected at having to take a back seat
for a while. Perhaps husbands can involve themselves in the
activities of the older children in such a way that they satisfy
one another's needs for attention in the midst of it.

Christian mothers have the privilege of saying, "Lord, I
feel so inadequate to meet the needs of all these children
and my husband. I ask You to give me the ability to show
forth Your love in such a way that no one will feel slighted."
The Lord will hear, and He will do it.

If there is no father in the home, the mother cannot give
the children the strength they need if she is lost in her own
needs:

"Poor me, I don't have an arm to lean on."

"I don't have anyone to help me make decisions."

"I'm having to rear these youngsters all by myself now,
and I'm just not capable of it."

Whether we express these things aloud or not, our
youngsters will hear them if that's how we feel. And what we
need to communicate to them is just the opposite:

"I am mother, I am capable."

"I am your protection, your mainstay, and I can do well
by you."

"I can support you, I can guide you, I can govern you, I
can take good care of you."

"I can love you so much and so wisely that you won't miss
a thing in life because you don't have a father."

If you are the head of a one-parent family, you have to
play a double role, so your child won't feel deprived. If you

tell your child, "If you had a daddy, you could enter the soap-box derby," you're not being fair to him. If he doesn't have a daddy to do such things with him, we have to find a substitute.

When other fathers and sons were going to the woods to chop down a tree at Christmas time, God always provided a Boy Scout leader or a responsible older teenage boy to take Danny out and do the same thing. He didn't stay at home because he didn't have a father, he just went tree-chopping with someone else.

One day, Danny came along as I was opening the trunk of my car to get out some filmstrips. Naturally, his curiosity was aroused.

"What's in those funny round boxes, mom—Christmas cookies?"

"No," I laughed. "They're some films we're going to use at a retreat this weekend."

"Movies? Oh, boy! What are they about?"

"Well, they're about problems with children. How children are affected by different things, like death, divorce—"

"Divorce? Gee! I want to see that one. I want to know how I was affected."

To me, that was heartwarming evidence that boys without fathers at home don't have to spend their lives suffering from being deprived of all the things that other boys can count on.

Trying to be mom and dad both to a child isn't easy, but it's possible. It helps if we understand at the beginning that at the times when we feel most ladylike, our kids might need us to oil their tricycles or wrestle on the grass. It's our responsibility to be sensitive to what they need when they need it, and to provide it for them where we can.

In one-parent family situations, the parent who lives with

the children can teach them to show affection for the absent parent.

At different times in their lives, both of my children have attempted to manipulate me by saying, "Mom, why do I have to write to dad? I don't know anything to say to him, and after all, he's not really part of our family anymore."

I could have agreed, and let their rejection of him feed my ego, but they needed to keep a close relationship with their father, and I knew it. Crossing him out of their lives would not be helpful to them.

"He is your father, he loves you, and he's good to you," I always told them. "You're going to write to him today." And they did it.

Children are to honor their father and their mother because God says so. The honoring is not based on what the parents do or do not do with their lives.

When both parents are a part of the household, an additional responsibility presents itself. Each needs to do all he can to hold the other parent in an attitude of respect before the children.

At a certain age, a child might say, "Mom, dad doesn't understand me, but you do." It's a big mistake to side with a youngster against his father. In two more years, the youngster might want to side with his father against his mother. The best thing to say is, "Well, honey, we're all different. I'm mother, and he's dad, and you're somebody else. But we're all in this family, and we need to work together and keep on loving each other." We can help our children to understand that there are no sides to a family, and that they have a responsibility to live in such a way as to benefit all members of it.

If children succeed in driving a wedge between mother

and father, they hate what they have done. A split between parents means the child is in control. He has to choose sides, and that's very frightening to a youngster.

If our child's father is a very passive person, who doesn't do the things a father ought to do for his children, we won't help our youngster by sitting back and waiting for something to happen, arguing, "Well, it's the father's place to do it. It's his fault that something isn't done."

We can't afford to justify our inaction that way or to waste energy on placing the blame. It really doesn't matter whose fault a particular lack is, the important thing is to do away with the lack. Sometimes, that will mean that one partner has to shoulder the entire responsibility while the other just sits there. It's work, but it's worth it to provide our children what they need.

4

Learning to Love

One of the duties of mothers mentioned in the Word of God is the duty to love their children. Titus 2:4 says that the older women are to teach the younger women "to be sober, to love their husbands, and to love their children."

When babies are little and helpless, mother love instinctively flows out like a river to meet their every need. As she meets the needs of her offspring, her own needs are met, and she's happy. But that's not where the story ends, with everyone living happily ever after in that kind of dependent relationship.

The child is to be weaned from total dependence on the parents as he grows old enough to handle some things for himself. The mother has to let the child learn to feed himself, to dress himself, to drink from a cup instead of a bottle.

Not so she can call long-distance and tell grandma, but
because children are meant to grow up to responsible
maturity of their own.

As children grow, they naturally begin to rebel against
what mother or daddy requires of them. If we don't learn to
love our youngsters in this new kind of relationship, life is
going to be full of negatives—a constant spanking, nagging,
scolding; a disappointment for all concerned.

We've all made the mistake of saying, "When you're a
good girl, mommy loves you." What we need to communicate is, "No matter what, mommy loves you." That's learned
love—love that keeps on loving whether the object of the
love behaves in acceptable or unacceptable ways. When a
child has misbehaved, he probably needs our love even
more than he does when he's in a right relationship with the
rest of the world.

If we take the wrong approach with our children, they
begin to think, "When I am pleasing, then I am loved."
Little girls who grow up with that notion believe that any
time they displease their husbands, their husbands no
longer love them.

Men believe the same things about their wives. It leads to
an attitude that says, "Gee, I'm going to be late getting
home. She'll be furious—she won't love me, because I've
displeased her." And so he doesn't go home at all. Instead,
he stops by a bar and finds someone who acts as if she'll love
him no matter what.

Divorce courts are full of people who were brought up to
believe that unacceptable behavior automatically results in a
withdrawal of love. For the non-Christian world, it's pretty
hopeless. But we who are children of God know that while
we were yet sinners, the Lord Jesus Christ loved us enough
to die for us. And we are called to follow His example, to

love others as He has loved us.

Having the model of God's love—which never leaves us or forsakes us, regardless of our behavior—we can pray that He will enable us to learn that kind of love for our children, and to communicate it to them.

Adults often say to me, "You know, when I look back on it now, I realize my mother and dad loved me, but I honestly didn't believe that when I was growing up."

That we love our children does not automatically mean that they know we love them. And they need to know it. Oh, *how* they need to know it.

When everything is going fine, and we're happy with life—not having any real battles—we probably show a measure of joy that our kids might interpret as love. But when everything is just like dynamite about to explode, it's a different story. If we and our kids are in the midst of a disagreement, they probably won't know that we still love them unless we verbalize it and follow up with loving actions.

In my home, we're very verbal about our feelings for one another. It's not at all unusual for Danny to be outside playing basketball, come in for a drink of water, yell "I love you, mom," and then slam out the door and be half a block away before I finish yelling my love back at him.

There are many non-verbal ways to communicate love, too. I've been in homes where I never heard anybody say, "I love you," and yet I could sense the love just thick in the air.

We can't ever afford to withhold love—or expressions of love—on account of bad behavior.

Many times, a little child will scream out in frustration, "You don't love me!" and the result is punishment, either physical or verbal:

"**Shame on you! You *know* I love you! Don't you?**"

"Yeah."

"Then don't ever, as long as you live, say such a terrible thing again!"

What comes through is a far cry from love, and the big scene sets up a defense mechanism in the child's mind that says, "Okay, I won't say it, but I'll sure think it."

A lot of behavioral problems stem from the fact that kids are still thinking things we have taught them not to say. True, we need to guide into appropriate times and places the things that need to be said, but when our youngster bursts out, "You don't love me!" it's time to take inventory.

Admittedly, there are kids who will try to manipulate us with this. Maybe we've had to correct them about something, and they've come up with, "You don't love me." If we catch them watching out of the corner of their eye to see how we'll take it, that's not a case of feeling unloved, it's a case of testing us to see if we're sucker enough to fall for their little scheme.

If we dissolve into something like, "Oh, honey, mommy doesn't—" apologizing all over the place and maybe backing down on the restricted privileges we were going to enforce, the child will think, "Chalk one up. I just won again." We'll have lost a lot. We can't fall for manipulation, but we can make sure our kids know we love them.

Debbie knew she was secure in my love, but sometimes, when I wouldn't permit her to have her way about something, she'd whimper, "You don't love me."

It was a little joke we had. I'd say, "That's how I prove I love you, by not letting you do what's not right." She knew it was true.

Kids are tremendous manipulators, and they seem to know us much better than we know them. They know our soft spots, and they know just how and when to nestle up and say, "Oh, mom, you're so great. You're the best cook in the whole wide world."

We probably ask, "What do you want, son?"

"Oh nothing. You're just great, that's all."

If there's a pause of any length, it's just so he can get up his nerve to ask, "Mom, can I go swimming this afternoon?"

After a build-up like that, how can we refuse? But rather than viewing that as manipulation, we can see it as a fun game we play. We probably let him go swimming. But if there is a good reason not to let him go, we don't change our mind for all the sweet-talk in the world.

Sometimes when we are nervous and upset about something—husband, wife, home, health, finances, job, neighbors, politics—our youngster comes running in the front door yelling, "Hey, mom!"

Instead of listening to what the "Hey, mom!" is about, we yell, "Shut that door, and get out of here!"

The child doesn't know what he's done wrong. He doesn't know that we are bearing other burdens and he just got blamed for them all. It makes him look at himself negatively, as a no-good, unloved, or at us as an unreasonable parent.

We all do stupid things like that sometimes, but the mistake can be remedied. The moment we become aware of what we've done, we can tell our child, "Honey, I'm sorry I was so ugly toward you. I was upset over something else, and I guess I took it out on you. But I shouldn't have done it. Please forgive me."

We may get a dirty look, but we'll have corrected an error.

Let's face it. We'll be wrong lots of times. We're human—we can't help it. But our kids won't respect us any less when we admit to them that we fall short of perfection. It can even make the bond of love stronger.

One day Danny and I had reached what seemed an absolute impasse in our relationship. I didn't know what was wrong, exactly, but I sensed that something was really bothering him about me. He hadn't had a kind word for me, or even a friendly look as far as I could recall, all day. It was too uncomfortable a situation to be ignored.

"Danny," I said, "do you know what a stroke is?"

He kind of glared at me, and his tone when he spoke was on the brink of real impatience.

"Yeah, mom, of course I know what a stroke is. It's something that happens to people and leaves their mouth kind of hanging open on one side—"

"No, son," I interrupted, "I'm talking about another kind of stroke, the kind psychologists talk about. To them, it's called a stroke when you pay a compliment or do a kindness for someone. When you do something that makes someone think you like them. When what you do or say meets their ego needs.

"I haven't had any strokes from you for a long time, Danny," I went on. "Why, I get more strokes from my son-in-law than I get from you—"

I could have bitten my tongue off as soon as the words were out of my mouth, but it wouldn't have done any good. They were said, I couldn't unsay them.

Danny just looked at me, I looked back at him, and we went our separate ways. The hurt was a solid wall between us.

Later, when I was getting ready to go to a meeting, Dan hung around as if he wanted to say something to me.

"Where are you going, mom?" He knew the answer to his question before he even asked it, but still, it was a start.

"To church, of course." I was still unbending.

"Well, would you like for me to drive you?"

It was a perfect opportunity for me to acknowledge his efforts to do something nice for me, but I was bristling inside, so I blew it.

"I'm quite capable of driving myself, thank you—"

When I saw the stricken look on his face, I woke up to the obvious—that he was ready to be reconciled to me. And suddenly, I was ready, too.

"Thanks for offering, Dan," I told him. "That was nice of you, and I really appreciate it." My voice had gotten kind of quivery by then, but when his six-foot-one frame bent to give me a goodbye hug, the lump in my throat melted.

We all blow it—time after time—in the business of bringing up our children. But if we keep our relationship to God up-to-date, He can—and will—mend all our mistakes.

Have you worried that you might spoil your youngsters by showing them too much love? Don't. Life is so short. Shower your kids with love. They'll get unspoiled soon enough, slapped around at a university, knocked around in service, kicked around in their first job. While they're still with us, we can give them tenderness, kindness, concern. We can let them know that no matter what they do, there's someone who loves them. I've seen adults get unspoiled rapidly, but I've never seen adults come into love suddenly who were deprived of love during their growing-up years.

Many children are burdened with low self-esteem. They believe their parents do not like them, because of all the negatives, negatives, negatives hurled at them all the time. "Don't do this; don't do that." We need to make them know that our actions are designed to ensure their happiness, not to deprive them of it. When they come to understand that, they'll be secure in the knowledge that because we love them we are doing the best we can for them.

5

Sibling Rivalry

Almost every parent who has more than one child has been aware at some time or another of feelings of jealousy between the children. Sibling rivalry is what it's called, and it can make life miserable for everybody.

Each child needs to feel secure in the love of his parents. No child can bear to feel left out, or even put in second place. It doesn't do any good for anyone to sputter to a child, "Look, I'm not being partial to your brother. It's all your imagination. I love you just as much as I love him." The child will not hear such protests. Instead, he will continue to react to what he believes is so. And we must deal with what the child *thinks* is so, not just with what we know is so.

After Danny was born, I came out of the hospital with

43

him and saw Debbie waiting in the back seat of the car.

"Here's your baby," I said to her as I put him in her lap. At the moment, the relationship that existed between them was a beautiful thing, but when Debbie was around eleven or twelve, something made her think I was showing partiality to Danny.

"I know you love me, but I think you love Danny more," she sniffed.

I sat down beside her on the couch and said, "Debbie, when daddy and I knew that we were going to have a baby, I never referred to it as 'the baby.' In all the letters that I wrote to your father when he was overseas, I always said, 'Debbie this' and 'Debbie that.' I was so sure we were going to have a girl—"

"Why?" she interrupted me, her eyes wide with surprise.

"Well," I said, "I wanted a girl, and I had prayed to God for a girl with black hair and brown eyes—just like you. When grandma came to stay with me before you were born, she did everything she could to talk me into thinking I might have a boy, but I wouldn't listen to her. Why, if God had sent a boy just then, I'd probably have sent him right back where he came from."

Debbie had to giggle at that, and I could see I was getting through. I went on to tell her about some of the little clothes I had bought for her and how proud I was to be her mother.

Now, Debbie didn't suddenly give me a lot of verbal feedback. She didn't throw her arms around me and cry, "Oh, mamma, now I really know you love me as much as you love Danny!" but her face gradually relaxed, and she looked happy. She knew then that I had looked forward to her before she was born.

No matter how hard we try, we can never completely and permanently do away with feelings of jealousy between our children. It is impossible. And our children will try to use our partiality, real or imagined, against us as a manipulative tool. If they get what they want from this manipulation, they'll employ it time and time again. Every time we have to say no to one of them, he'll say, "Yeah. It's because you like so and so better'n you like me."

A child will try to make us back down. But if we do, we've had it. We have to be on guard against falling into this trap. At the same time, we have to be aware of our children's need for reassurance.

A friend of mine one day noticed that her daughter, who was usually very outgoing and cheery, had become withdrawn and sulky and had taken to spending a lot of time in her room. She asked her what the problem was.

Her daughter shrugged. "Nothing's the matter. What makes you think something's the matter?"

"Something has to be the matter," my friend replied. "You haven't been yourself lately, and even now I can tell you're angry. I'd like to help if I can." She just stood there, and finally her daughter came out with it.

"Well," she said, tears forming in her eyes, "you let Johnny go to camp last week, and you won't even let me spend the night with Sarah. Things like this seem to happen all the time. Mom, you like Johnny better than you like me."

My friend was able to explain to her daughter what her reasons were behind her decisions, which led into a real heart-to-heart talk. She made certain that her explanation brought out that she *did* love her—so much that she could hardly stand it—and that her refusal of permission was for her good. She was careful not to downgrade her son Johnny in the process, of course; she knew that there was a chance that, if *that* happened, her daughter would lord it over him, and then she'd have another broken heart to mend.

In certain cases, we may actually *be* partial to one child over another. If that happens, we need to be alert not to go to the opposite extreme in order to compensate.

This is especially a danger in homes in which retarded children are growing up. In such cases, mothers tend to overcompensate. At its worst, this kind of over-reaction can literally destroy the potential of the "normal" children in the home, since it deprives them of the mothering they need. In the natural, the mother may prefer them, but because she devotes so much of her attention to her one retarded child, they feel rejection.

Another feeling of rejection seems to be a natural part of growing up. At about age eleven, a lot of kids decide that they were probably adopted into their family. They think they don't look like the rest of the kids, and they know for a certainty that they're not treated as well as the others. This is a typical manifestation of the age of insecurity. An extra measure of love from us will usually effect a cure.

Taking thoughtful inventory of our actions, maybe we realize that at a certain stage we are being overly indulgent toward the child who's slower than another mentally, who finds it harder to get along in school, who has a physical disability, or who doesn't have many friends. An honest appraisal forces us to agree that our partiality hasn't really helped the youngster as much as it has fed our own need to be needed. In fact, the result has probably been further rejection of the child by his brothers and sisters, making the problems worse instead of better for them and for us.

If we have a youngster who from birth has been an I-can-do-it-myself creature, we may have a tendency to turn too much attention to the less-outgoing child in order to assuage our own feelings of rejection by the independent one. It is important for parents to be aware of and to guard against this in themselves if they want their children to love one another.

We may be more comfortable around one of our youngsters than another because one is more sensitive to our needs. He just seems to know when we're feeling out of sorts, and he leaves us alone. Not only that, but he runs interference for us with the other kids, telling them "Leave mom alone today. Can't you see she's tired?"

When we're sick, that child is the one who cleans up the dirty dishes and then comes in and waits on us, all unasked. Sometimes our subconscious says to us, "That kid likes me better; he loves me more than the other kids do." Without being aware of it, we may begin to show partiality toward him.

It is easy to play favorites and to find excuses for it, but it's dangerous business for the peace and harmony of the home.

How can we divide our attention among our youngsters in a way that will be most beneficial? We can begin by giving our attention to the child who is most needy at the moment. Sometimes we can involve two or more children at the same time in what we're doing. When we have to make an arbitrary choice, wherever possible we can decide in favor of the teenager. We may have years left to deal with the younger child, but what we don't give the teenager now, he might not be around to get later.

Suppose we start making a cake with one youngster and the other comes in demanding attention. If we say, "Okay, Susie will mix it, but you can pour it into the pans," Susie may very well leave the scene. Her attitude may be, "Forget it. If this isn't going to be special—just you and me, mom— who cares about making a dumb cake?"

Making the cake was not what was special to Susie in the first place. The cake-making was just an excuse for being with mom for an exclusive dose of her attention for a little while. Admittedly, the youngster we turn away may be out of sorts for a while, but we can make it up to him later. Including him when the other is not welcoming his participation hurts them both, and we're worse off than when we started.

We can say to the one who wants to intrude, "No, you can't help just now. Susie and I are doing this. Next time, maybe you and I will make a cake." We might suggest something the other child can do instead, and be firm about it.

The resolution of this conflict is actually helpful to the child who first needed the attention. Our attitude says to her, "See, I am meeting your needs exclusively right now." When she is satisfied that she is the center of our attention, then she might become more willing to include everybody in the picture. We have to be careful not to let a child feel that everything is mass treatment and that there's never anything special just for him or her.

When one youngster has provoked another to wrath, we don't just try to stop the fight. We try to find out what really happened. Then, we try to interpret their reactions to them. When we explain to each of them why the other felt as he did, why he reacted as he did, and that *he'd* have reacted in the same way if the roles had been reversed, we're helping them to understand themselves and the other guy. That paves the way for a modification of behavior the next time a similar situation arises.

Little boys like to tease, but if we can get them to understand that they wouldn't like for someone else to tease them, they'll begin to come out of their tormenting phase.

If we can get them to look with us at both sides of the conflict, to consider which side they'd rather have been on, the air will be clear again. Then they can start a new fight—without anything left over from the first one.

If both children are not present when we learn about trouble between them—maybe an argument about a dump truck in the sandpile—we can afford to make complete identification with the one who is with us. "Yeah, I know how you must feel. I'd want to have my turn first, too."

He will go flying out to tell his brother, "Mom says she doesn't blame me." Then the second child will come in, and we'll have a chance to take his side, this time. Both kids will feel comforted and more secure than ever. When they see that there's no reason for them to be jealous about our judgments, that each has our undivided sympathy, the rivalry that starts so many fights will be temporarily knocked out of the picture.

In cases where sibling quarrels are just a bid for attention, ignoring the situation can be the best solution to it.

A woman told me about her daughters who began bickering the moment they got home from school each day. She had tried to settle their arguments so many times that she was tired of it. One day, she just went into another room when the girls began to quarrel and acted as if she didn't hear what was going on. Finally, their curiosity got the best of them, and they peeked through the doorway to see if their mother was still among the living. Seeing her calmly sitting in a chair reading a book, they were astonished.

"Mamma!" one of them cried, "you don't care if Sally *kills* me!"

Sally cried, "Mamma, you don't care if Laura kills *me!*"

Mamma turned the page of the magazine on her lap and looked up to answer.

"That's right, Laura! That's right, Sally; I *don't* care."
Mamma went back to her reading, the girls looked at one
another in open-mouthed amazement and were soon giggling together happily.

That a youngster becomes old enough to go away to
college doesn't mean he no longer needs his parents for
anything except money. A mother of a large family told me
about her twenty-year-old son who came in wanting her
attention one day when she had her hands full taking care
of a little one. He could see that she was busy, but he just
stood in the doorway, his presence demanding her attention anyway.

Frustrated at being torn in two directions at once, the
mother complained, "Son, can't you see that I have all I can
do to take care of this situation just now?"

Well, he saw, of course, but he stood his ground for a
moment before turning to go out.

"All right, mom," he said. "But it seems like you're always
too busy for me. I need a mother, too, you know."

The mother got the message loud and clear, and she was
careful to be all ears the next time he favored her with his
presence.

We should never let our child feel rejected, even when he
is old enough to be more or less on his own, when he gets
married or goes away to college. We can't afford to divorce
ourselves from the child who may be coming home only for
occasional weekends. We do all we can to keep the family
unity, to encourage the youngsters to feel part of one
another.

We try to arrange to be at home when the child who lives
away drops in. We make ourselves available to meet his
needs. We don't turn his old room into a guest room the first

week he's sleeping away from home. We don't move his things to a storage closet or smaller bedroom just because he isn't around much anymore. We let him keep on sharing the number-one spot with his brothers and sisters, let him know he's still an important member of the family setup. That knowledge is vital to him.

Another important thing for us to realize in preserving the closeness of the family relationship with our grown-up children is that we don't have to become a slave to our visiting-for-the-weekend college student. Sure, he'll bring in a loaded laundry bag of dirty clothes, but if we've brought him up right, he'll remember how to use the washer and dryer for himself. It will be good for him to resume his usual chores when he's home for a few days. What better time for mom and daughter to visit than when they are washing and drying the dishes together? Or for father and son to have real fellowship than when they're raking the scattered fallen leaves in the front yard on Saturday afternoon or checking to see what's wrong under the hood of the car?

We don't always have to blow the budget on a standing rib roast for our visiting older children either. They'll feel more like they're still really a part of the family if we serve them canned soup or a peanut butter sandwich once in a while, just like in the old days. It's the quality of love we give them, not the filet mignon, that makes them secure in their place in the family.

One mother found herself with two daughters away in college at the same time. Both were in nearby schools so they were able to come home almost every weekend. There was no *need* for a lot of letters back and forth, because the family would be together for the weekend almost before a letter could be delivered. In emergencies, it was even possible for the mother to get through to the girls via dormitory telephone.

One of the girls took the matter of an empty mailbox in her stride, realizing her parents were busy with many other things. But the other girl was upset about her empty mailbox and insisted that her mom write to her often.

Well, at first, the mom felt quite indignant that her daughter was so demanding of her. Then she recognized a real need in that child to have the assurance of family love in her new away-from-home life. Disciplining herself to write her daughter a note of some kind every single day for a week, the mother found her *own* attitude toward the *child's* attitude softening. What she began as a grit-my-teeth-and-get-it-over-with chore became a time of real blessing to her.

It seems to be a law of life that whenever we do something to meet the need of another person, love for others grows in us. Expression of love is needed, and everybody is benefited from poured-out love. And as we submit ourselves in love to one another, our own needs are met.

6

Your Kids and Their Peers

In the first and second grade, it's very common for little boys and girls to be in love with each other. Whenever I noticed that Danny had a new little girl's name inked on his hand, I'd ask him to tell me about her. His sweethearts were always blonde, always clever, really talented. Because I encouraged him to tell me about his girlfriends in the beginning, he was free to tell me about them later when the romances broke up. We kept the door of communication open between us. At first, his explanation was always an ego-saving declaration that *he* dumped *them*, but later he came to the point of being able to say, "Jennifer turned me over for Steve."

"Oh?" I said. "How come?"

"I dunno—I guess maybe she doesn't like tall boys."

53

Being jilted didn't give him any complexes. It was a normal part of life.

Often first graders bit by the love bug will exchange telephone numbers with one another. It's interesting to eavesdrop on these conversations. A little girl will dial her boyfriend, and he'll be thrilled to death that she called but so embarrassed he can't say anything better than a grumpy, "Well, what did you call *me* for?"

Instead of answering his question, she'll say, "Well, I've got to go now," and slam the phone down in his ear.

This is standard operating procedure for peer with peer. They understand each other. The kids don't call to say anything in the first place; they're just making contact. Later, their conversations will be more than long enough to make up for these early short ones.

Nobody seems to care whether or not a sixth-grade boy is interested in girls, but when he returns to school for the seventh grade, he has to be a real swinger or get laughed out of school.

"How many girls have you kissed?" one kid will ask another.

"Oh, I don't know," the other guy will answer, as nonchalant as you please. "Probably around seventeen or eighteen."

Neither of them has ever *touched* a girl, but they've got to talk as if they're seasoned lovers. They are pressured to use a whole new vocabulary and to be in a whole new life style to be a big man on campus.

The pretending goes along fine until the boy goes out with a girl as caught up in social pressures and as ignorant as he is. He doesn't know but what she expects of him the same thing the boys expect, and she doesn't know any better either. He starts moving in on her because he think it's expected of him, she doesn't know enough to stop things before they get out of hand, and trouble takes over. In the seventh grade! A lot of it is the fault of grownups.

When Debbie was in the sixth grade, her teacher said to me, "Your daughter is doing beautifully academically, but she is behind socially." I knew what she was talking about, so I smiled and nodded my head.

"When Debbie first came to this class," the teacher went on, "every boy had a crush on her, but she doesn't seem to have any interest in boys. I'm a little concerned about this, Mrs. Tompkins, aren't you?"

"Not a bit."

The teacher looked at me as if I had suddenly sprouted two heads or something.

"Aren't you concerned?" she wanted to know. "The average mother is worried sick if her little girl in the sixth grade isn't boy-crazy."

"Well, I guess I'm not average, then," I told her. "I'm not only not concerned—I'm *glad* Debbie isn't boy-crazy yet. She has plenty of time for that later on."

The teacher just stared at me, then shook her head.

Dating pressure is on today's teenagers. Everywhere they turn, someone asks them, "Do you have a date for the party? Who are you going with?"

And yet when I talk to the boys by themselves, I invariably find that they enjoy playing basketball, building models, or playing chess, *not* going out with girls.

One time when my daughter was complaining about having nothing to do, I suggested, "Why don't you just call up a bunch of kids and have them over for popcorn?"

Her response was mingled incredulity and sarcasm.

"Now wouldn't that just be a *ball!*" she said, shaking her

head and looking at me as if she thought I'd lost my marbles.

"I think the kids would enjoy it," I told her. But she
wouldn't be persuaded. Later I checked it out to see if I was
really that much behind the times. I asked some kids sepa-
rately, out of earshot of the others, "Say, if we called you up
tonight and invited you over to eat popcorn and watch TV,
would you like that?"

"Gee, that'd be great! What time can I come?" they asked.
The individual response was unanimously in favor of the
idea, but collectively, they were afraid someone would make
fun of them.

Pressure from teachers, parents, and peers doesn't let
children be children long enough. They have to put away
childhood and play at adult roles before they're ready. If we
encourage them in that direction, we're guilty of stealing
from them some important joys of childhood.

Even thirteen-year-old kids who have just gone into
junior high school are considered adult and are called on to
make important decisions that will affect their whole lives.
In many cases, they go at the same time from being the
oldest students in a grade or junior high school to being the
youngest in a high school.

Boys and girls are belittled and made fun of if they aren't
in rebellion against the establishment. They're ridiculed if
their clothes aren't sloppy enough, and they're held up to
scorn if they do their homework.

Feelings of insecurity and inadequacy and uncomforta-
bleness, among both boys and girls, multiply. They can't
feel they are measuring up either socially or academically.
Their world is actually in conflict with itself.

Maybe we encourage our child to do the "in" thing, no
matter how reluctant he feels about it, or maybe we go to the

other extreme and insist that our darling keep on wearing little-girl bobby socks and pigtails. Either way, we and our child are in for mountainous frustration.

Where should the line be drawn about how far we let our kids follow their peers?

The first secret is in finding a balance between the extremes.

One mother who has an unusually good relationship with her teenagers said to me, "I stay alert to their spiritual growth because, to me, this makes a difference in how far I'm going to allow them to follow the crowd. Little things, like hair styles, I can go along with."

For her, getting used to long hair on boys was easy. For me, it was tough, because I equated long hair on guys with rebellion.

Another mother told me, "I try to encourage my children to apply Christian principles in matters of dress for themselves. We talk about such things as, 'How modest should a Christian be?' rather than laying down the law and saying, 'You will not wear thus and such a thing because I don't like it, and that's that.' "

Her approach was wise. To start with, a child who is wearing what he likes, something in which he feels comfortable, something that doesn't set him apart from the crowd, is going to be a lot happier, better behaved, more secure and stable than one who feels awkward and out of place because of what he has on.

Parents who don't observe their own children in a group setting are often not aware of how important style is to a youngster. It's easy for an adult to say, "Your skirt is too short," or "You've got to get your hair cut." But the kids who are set radically apart from their peers will die all day at school because of a too long skirt or too short hair. It is important for us to try to understand our children's point of view, to see things their way if possible.

Security among their peers is important to children of any age. If what they want to wear, or how they want to style their hair, is basically harmless, it's well enough to try to go along with their desires.

There isn't anything I loathe more than high-top tennis shoes. They look abominable on everybody, but that's the only kind of shoe my son would wear to school at one time. He had a narrow foot, so I had to special-order his shoes, and I didn't always get around to it as soon as I should have. I remember one day when he had a couple of big holes in the soles of his tennis shoes, but he had a perfectly lovely pair of brown loafers in the closet.

"Danny, why don't you wear your loafers to school today?" I asked him.

His tone of voice told me I must have crawled out from under a rock somewhere.

"You gotta be kidding!" he exploded. "What do you think I am, some kind of a creep? Nobody wears loafers to *school.* I'd rather go barefooted than be caught dead in loafers."

He was so upset about it, I let him go to school wearing his ragged tennis shoes, their soles flopping almost off. It made me feel as if maybe I ought to apply for public welfare. But if I had insisted that he wear his good shoes instead of his decrepit ones, it wouldn't have been because I was concerned that he might take cold from getting his socks wet. It would have been my pride showing.

We need to check our own motives once in a while and encourage our children to examine theirs, as well as the effect on other people of how they dress.

One day Debbie went to the gym wearing a pair of cutoff blue jeans. When she came home, she asked me, "Mom, are these pants too tight on me?"

Because I was so accustomed to seeing all Debbie's friends in skintight pants, I hadn't given any particular thought to hers.

"Oh," I said, "I don't know that they're any tighter than anybody else's. Why do you ask?"

"Well," she said, "I just wondered, because while I was in the gym, five different people came along and swatted me on the seat."

"That tells you what you wanted to know, then, doesn't it, Deb?" We both laughed, she nodded, and I could tell that at fifteen she had learned, on her own, that following the crowd wasn't always worth what it cost.

As our youngsters mature, they will begin to weigh one thing against another, to decide for themselves how far they want to follow the gang. When our child comes home and says everybody is going to a place that is anti-God and anti-us, we can say, "Everybody *isn't* going, because you're not," but in less vital matters, we don't have to be so dogmatic.

In the past, Christians have sometimes defeated their own purposes by being unreasonably extreme in their views. When I was growing up, I was ridiculed in gym class because my religion did not permit me to learn the two-step. My mother and father made such a scene over the dance classes in public school that kids and teachers alike made fun of me. I had to make written reports to the teacher instead of participating in the fun.

Being punished for something that was not my fault made me really bitter. It did me far more damage than learning the two-step would have done.

We need to look at the long-range effect of our parental actions. As Christian parents, we have to draw a fine line without letting the kids see the chalk, without setting up stumbling blocks. We can let them be a part of everything that will not harm them spiritually. We can let them feel, "I'm one of the gang. I am accepted."

Then the no-nos, the things we can't allow—drinking beer, smoking pot—will not make them feel estranged from all their friends. Departure from the crowd on a single issue or two doesn't become a traumatic thing in their peer relationships unless we've insisted on a total separation act all along, always pulling our youngsters to ourselves, telling them, "We're better than other people. We're different."

The truth is that we *are* different, but our little kid in grade school is not prepared to hear it. He wants to be liked. He wants to like others.

We can handle the situation for our grade-schoolers by saying, "Sure we like the other kids. We like the games, the sports, the fun. We like this, that, and the other. It's just this one thing we don't like."

I never suggested to my daughter that she not dance. But after she had attended two teenage dances, she came to me and said that she didn't want to go again.

"All those flashing lights and loud music gave me a headache," she said.

"Debbie, why do you think the other kids enjoy the dances?" I asked her.

"I don't know," she shrugged. We talked for a while about why her reaction might be different from that of the other kids. We decided the difference was that the Holy Spirit in her was grieved, because the atmosphere of the dance did not glorify God.

Debbie's decision about attending the dances was a lasting thing with her, because it came from her and not from me.

Christian kids *are* different from their unChristian peers

because they have Christ inside them. Older kids can understand that and accept their being different and liking different things from other kids. It becomes a positive factor in their own eyes, not something that drags them down.

How we react in the face of inevitable peer conflicts teaches our child a lot about proper relationships.

The indulgent parent who always sides with his own youngster when he comes in with a problem with one of his friends is teaching him that he does not have a responsibility to get along with others. If a friend displeases him for any reason, the youngster knows that he can run to daddy and mommy, and they will take his side of it.

The less indulgent parent is likely to go to the other extreme and always blame his own youngster when there is a disagreement on the playground. If we always say "Son, it's your fault," we are teaching our child that the peer will always win over him, that there is never going to be any justice in his favor, and that he must, therefore, be basically inferior to other people.

Even with preschoolers, it makes a difference how you handle their peer relationships.

Danny came in crying one day. "I lost my favorite marble," he wailed, "and those kids are bigger'n me."

My instinctive reaction was to go out and beat up the big kids for taking a marble from my little kid, but I asked for a little clarification first. Out the window, I could see some bigger boys kneeling around a circle scratched on the sidewalk.

"What do you mean you lost your favorite marble? Did those big boys take it?"

"Well, not exactly," he sniffed. "There's this game, and—"

He explained keepies to me, just as if I hadn't grown up playing keepies with my four brothers.

"Danny," I told him, "sometimes when you're playing for keeps, you'll win a lot of marbles from some other poor kid who is going to go away crying. Other times, you'll be the one to lose a lot of marbles. Every time you gamble, something like that could happen. That's just the way it is. If you can't learn to be a good loser, you'd better not play for keeps."

From that day, Danny permitted himself to gamble with *some* of his marbles, but not with all of them. He gave himself an allotment, disciplined himself to stay within it, and didn't expect any pity from me when he lost.

Danny grew up knowing what to gamble with and what not to gamble with. He became comfortable with the truth, "If you're going to gamble, you can lose." He learned to take the consequences. In my opinion, that was a lot better than setting him apart from his peers by telling him he couldn't play for keeps.

At times, it may be necessary for us to teach our youngsters' friends something when we want them to behave in ways that are acceptable to us.

One mother told of a trio of economically disadvantaged children who spent their afternoons playing in her yard. The kids would come in the house for emergency trips to the bathroom, urgent drinks of water, and the like. Each trip was used as an excuse to ask for an apple from the fruit bowl. Seeing that their example couldn't be helpful to her child, who had been taught it was not polite to ask for things, the mother decided to do some instructing herself. One day, instead of handing out apples when they were asked for, she explained to the children that asking was impolite, and that they should not do it again.

That day, she didn't give the children anything except the lecture. Her own child paid close attention. For a few days, the boys didn't ask for an apple, but the woman instructed her son to offer one to each of them. He got a reinforced lesson in sharing and in good manners at one stroke.

Where our youngster associates with children from families whose standards are very different from ours, we have to be watchful to discover whether or not our child is being adversely influenced by them. If we see that he is incapable of saying no to another youngster who is forever in trouble for setting fires, stealing, or vandalism, we may have to deny our child the privilege of playing with the troublemaker. When we do this, however, we have to keep in mind that excluding one undesirable from our child's circle of playmates does not eliminate the possibility of all wrong companionship. Isolation from bad influence is not by any means the total answer to developing good character.

It is true that our youngster might have a very good sense of right and wrong for himself and still be led into doing wrong things through the influence of peer pressure. However, that our youngster does a wrong thing to please his peers doesn't necessarily mean he thinks the wrong thing is right. He may be hating himself, dying of guilt, all the time he is engaged in the wrong action.

Group pressure can make him temporarily violate his own standards—but not forever. A child who has real security will come back to family standards for himself as he becomes mature enough to buck the crowd and stand up for what he believes in.

Sometimes when kids are asking to do something they know is against our principles, they're asking on account of peer pressure, and they really want us to say no so they can have an out. But they don't want to admit that to us. Such an admission would be belittling to them. They're not quite adult enough not to care that they're *not* following the crowd, and they're not quite adult enough in themselves to choose not to follow.

We'll never find out their whys by instant moralizing on the subject. To say, "You know better," is to slam the door on finding out their motivations and helping them grow up into self-discipline.

One night at dinner, my daughter announced that she was going to read a certain salacious novel. I saw her watching for my reaction, wondering whether I'd blow up or what I'd do. Because we had guests (that fact had entered into her calculations, too), I didn't make an issue of it, just let it go with a nonchalant, "Oh?" and we went on with dinner. Later, I went to her room to talk about her announcement. I hadn't read the book myself, but knew from a review that the book was not recommended reading for teenage girls. Instead of handing her a stamp of disapproval, however, I began to question her.

"This book you're planning to read, Debbie, what's it about?"

"I don't know," she shrugged, "but all the kids are reading it."

Just as I thought. Peer pressure. To have read the dirty novel was the status symbol of the hour.

"Go ahead and read it if you want to," I said, keeping my attitude low-key, "but I understand it's a filthy book, and I don't think you'll enjoy it."

I didn't give her anything to react against, and she never read the book. Our open communication didn't forbid her reading it. She wasn't left feeling that she had to rebel against authority and sneak it in the house. Free to make her own decision, she made a mature one.

What should we do when our children want to go along with the gang and watch TV programs or movies of which we don't approve? With preteens, if we've thought it through, we can be firm in our decision, regardless of what they think. But for teenagers, it is well to examine their reasons for wanting to watch certain off-limits programs or movies.

If our child goes to such a movie, comes home and talks to us about it and then doesn't express a desire to go again, we can let the matter drop. Chances are that some need within him has been satisfied by seeing the movie, and no harm has been done. But if the same child wants to go repeatedly to see movies we think will not be good for him, we might ask, "John, what is it you get out of going to movies like that?" By phrasing our question in that way, we encourage him to examine his own motives.

I don't believe in simply telling older kids they can't go. I've seen too many become real addicts to such things the minute they get away from home and out from under parental watchfulness. It's best for them to be exposed while they're still at home where we can guide them.

We can't prevent our youngsters from seeing violence. We live in a violent world. Kids must learn to cope with it.

Suppose we keep our teenage boys from seeing violence on the screen—it would take a miracle, but it might be done—and then, in their upper teens, they get sent away to war? They may be exposed to violence first-hand, up close, not make-believe but real. Such kids come home from war ready for the mental hospitals. They may stay there a long time.

At one time, Debbie was interested in a certain TV show she had seen at a friend's house, and so we watched it together a few times. The humor on the program was very subtle and tremendously risque in many areas. I noticed that Deb laughed each time I did. Just checking, I asked her, "Do you know what that meant?"

She hadn't understood any of it.

There was a day when naivete was considered precious, but that's not true any more. It's actually dangerous sometimes. Our kids may be belittled and taken advantage of if they don't know the score. Whenever possible, I've let my kids be in the know, even explaining risque jokes to Debbie.

Living in a pretense world is not helpful for your kids or mine. Today, more than ever before, they have to know "where it's at" in order to survive. They'll be living in a world with their peers, whether we like it and approve or not. Instead of burying our heads in the sand and insisting that they do likewise, we need to equip them with all they need to cope successfully with the real world around them.

7

Your Kids and School

Counseling a six-year-old one day, I asked him, "How's everything at school?"

"All right," he muttered, without any enthusiasm.

"Just 'all right'?" I asked him. "What's the matter? Are you having problems at school?"

"No, no problems."

"Getting good grades?"

"Yeah."

"Like your teacher?"

"Yeah."

"How about the playground? Are you getting along with the kids at recess?"

"Sure. Everything's fine at recess."

"Well," I said, "I guess I must be crazy, then, because I have a feeling that something's wrong at school."

"You do?" His passivity had sparked to life. "That's funny, cause my mom thinks there's something wrong at school, too."

In all innocence, probably, the mother might have looked at an assignment in new math and fumed, "That's a stupid way for them to teach you."

She probably didn't realize that every word she spoke or didn't speak about school would be indelibly registered in the mind of her youngster.

I remember the first time I was confronted with the new math. Danny had come home almost in tears because he had so many division problems to do for homework.

"Don't worry about it, Danny," I had told him. "Mother will help you, and we'll get them done in a hurry."

He sat down at the table and opened his book to the page of problems. I started writing down numbers on a piece of paper, saying "That is the answer to that, and that is the answer to that, and—" I was doing the short-division problems in my head, of course.

Danny took the pencil ever so gently out of my hand, shaking his head as if to say, "Isn't it a pity. And she *looks* so intelligent."

What he said was, "Mom, I'm sorry, but that is not the way to work the problems." He started writing numbers down the side of the page, and then adding them all up—or something. Being totally in the dark, and overwhelmingly frustrated and embarrassed, I let my exasperation out in words.

"Danny, it's utterly ridiculous for you to have to put five numbers down there and then put that thing at the top. You

can work the whole thing out in your head. All you've got to
do is—"

Well, he had to do it the school's way, of course, and I
noticed that he didn't talk to me about his math homework
any more. My exasperated statement had communicated to
him, "You have to make a choice between mother's way and
the school's way." He had chosen. And I had learned a
lesson—not in arithmetic: I couldn't afford to put my
youngster in the midst of a conflict between me and the
school.

I don't want to put up a wall of separation between me
and anything in my youngsters' lives. It's my responsibility
to guide them, and I can't if I don't know what is going on. I
have a responsibility to keep the door open for communication in every area, because they're emotionally involved
with me, and what I say matters to them. Kids can find
themselves in the uncomfortable middle whenever teacher
says one thing and mother says another. But if their emotional needs are properly and fully met by parents in the
home, they don't have to carry over any emotional response
to what they're learning at school in philosophy, social
studies, literature, etc. Their attitude there can be a de-
tached, "That's what the teacher believes, so that's how I'll
answer the question on the test." They can take it or leave it,
in perfect freedom, without frustration.

Debbie was exposed to a little bit of teaching about evolution when she was in junior high school. When she came
home from school one day, she tried to shock me with it, but
I didn't shock.

"Boy! No kidding?" I exclaimed, when she told me that
her teacher said that man was descended from an ape.
"What if it's true?"

She laughed and told me what she knew that proved that

evolution *couldn't* be true. She had already learned, at the deepest levels of her being, that in the beginning, God made us. Because Debbie was secure in her emotional relationship with me, the false teaching at school didn't throw her. It didn't cause any confusion in her mind. In any subject with emotional overtones, the highest authority is mom and dad.

It is up to us to maintain such a rapport with our youngsters that they will tell us what they learn from others so we can help them cope with any truth or error they encounter.

One mother called her child to the window one day to show her a rainbow.

"Isn't the rainbow beautiful, honey?" the mamma said. "And you remember from our Bible story book that it's a sign of God's promise that He'll never again destroy the world with a flood."

The child nodded in agreement, but added, "At school today they told me that the rainbow is really just the colors made through the raindrops when the sun is shining."

The mother was able to explain that the scientific explanation was correct but that it was God who made the laws of science work just the way they do. The child was able to accept both aspects of knowledge about rainbows without any conflict.

It is obvious that we won't know as much as our youngsters do about some of the things that are taught in the schools today. We don't have to pretend that we know something we don't. That does more harm than good. But there isn't any loss at all in a good parent-child relationship when the parent says to the youngster, honestly, "Son, I don't know the answer to that one." My youngsters have never torn me apart or wanted to leave home because I gave them an "I don't know" answer. We can't know everything.

When I was in school, I hated history. By the skin of my teeth and my mother's prayers, I got by. I didn't care what happened in the dim distant past, I insisted. I wanted to put all my attention on living for today.

When Debbie brought her history book home from school, she asked me a question, and I had to tell her that I didn't know the answer.

"Then why do I have to learn this stupid stuff?"

The answer to that was easy, I thought.

"Well, Debbie, you have to learn it because that's what they teach you in school, and later, when your own youngster comes home, you're going to have to know—"

She interrupted me with the truth.

"How come I have to know? You didn't know. You couldn't tell me."

She had me there. And at that point, I was tempted to get on my high horse and yell at her, "Yeah, that's right! I don't know it—and that's exactly why you're going to learn it!" But I'd have lost valuable ground if I'd done that. I'd have set up resentment and rebellion in her.

That day, I was blessed to do the right thing for a change. I said to her, "Debbie, I know exactly how you feel. You'll just have to do the same thing I did. Read your assignments, get your homework in, and pay close attention in class. It won't last forever."

I didn't have to pretend I liked history. I didn't have to pretend I understood it. I didn't have to pretend I thought it was good for Debbie to learn it. But she had to take it because it was part of the school curriculum.

A true teacher cares about children. She spends more time with them than we do, and needs us to support her in every way we can. The teacher is not always right, but then, neither are we.

There may be times when we have to go to see our child's teacher about some problem area. We can't afford to go until we have stopped being angry. A display of anger could cause the teacher to close her mind to what we might have to say. If we calm down first, and *then* go to see the teacher, she'll be able to hear our side of it, and we can hear her side of it, too. It is important for us to understand her point of view as well as to express our own. Until we talk with her, we've heard only the side of the story that gives all of the benefit of doubt to our youngster. The whole truth might present a very different picture. We might even be persuaded that our child, instead of being a perfectly innocent bystander, was actually a ringleader in the trouble.

If our child has a teacher who punishes the whole class for the misbehavior of one or a few members of it, we can use the situation to teach our youngster that his very presence with someone misbehaving makes him a party to it.

I've told my son, "If you're with a group of boys who rob a store, and you don't even know they're going to do it, but you're sitting in the car when they're picked up, you'll be taken before the authorities along with the rest of them."

"But, mom," he argued, "I can't *not* go to school. I *have* to be there with everybody, good or bad. There's no way I can get out of associating with them."

"True," I agreed. "In school, you have no choice, but wherever you do have a choice—"

He got the point, and he has lived by it, knowing that he has to be careful in his choice of friends, because he will have to share the blame for any wrongdoing.

If, instead of using this kind of situation as a tool to teach our child something he needs to know, we take an extreme negative approach, saying, "Punishing everybody is not right. I agree with you, son, that the teacher has no right to make everybody stay after school just because a few of them did something wrong," we are keeping our youngster from learning a very important lesson.

If our youngsters sense in us a lack of concern for their school—if we never join the PTA and we're never interested enough to look over the test papers they bring home—they lose interest, too.

Some parents protest, "That's ridiculous! I don't have time to go to any old PTA meeting." There is a way to handle that, too. In our town, PTA meetings were always on Tuesday night, and that was my church choir night. There was no way I could be in both places at once, so when the kids brought home the little PTA membership form every year, I filled it out, gave them my dollar for membership, and explained, "Now, you know that mother can't go to the meetings, because it's my choir night, but you tell the people I'll be glad to furnish refreshments for their socials or do anything else I can to help."

By using that approach, I kept them from thinking, "Mom doesn't care. She isn't interested in my school." They knew I *was* interested.

If our child complains of being bored to death at school, we shouldn't ignore it. Boredom at school is an indication of one of two extremes—either our child is so far ahead of his class that there's nothing to challenge him, or he's so far behind he has no hope of ever catching up. In either case, we can do something about it.

I've never found a school yet that was not willing to cooperate when the administrators knew that a problem existed and what the problem was. Sometimes they put the

bored youngster in a higher class, one better suited to his
capabilities. Sometimes they assigned to him a challenging
project guaranteed to stimulate a youngster's interest in a
subject. Other times they provided the necessary tutorial
help to enable a youngster to catch up with his class.

Praise and reward are tremendous incentives for learning. Teachers are using it more and more, and we parents
should, too. When we look through papers brought home
from school, even papers with A's on them, do we automatically inflict some form of negative reaction on the youngster?

Do we begin with a smile, saying, "These are really *good*
papers. I'm proud of you!" but then spoil it with an almost
threatening, "Do you have any homework for tonight?"

Or do we say, "Oh, Johnny, I'm *so* pleased with these," but
put him down with, "They're so much better than those
awful things you brought home last week"?

None of that is praise and reward. It is barely a momen-
tary acceptance of something the child tried hard to achieve
to please us. No wonder he gets discouraged and thinks,
"What's the use of trying? I can't please dad no matter what
I do."

When there is anything good for which we can commend
our children, we can *dwell* on it. We can let our praise and
reward be full of accentuating the positive. There'll be
plenty of time later for dealing with the negatives, for
dishing out warnings. If we use the positive moments for
undiluted positives, we'll find ourselves getting more and
more of them.

When Johnny has succeeded for a change, we don't need
to cut him down. He needs building up.

If our child comes in on time, we shouldn't take it for
granted with an almost negative, "Well, I'm glad to see that

at least you got in on time for a change." That doesn't make him—or us—feel good. It makes everybody feel bad.

We can be enthusiastic when he walks in according to schedule.

"Hey! Ten o'clock on the button. Right on time. I appreciate that."

We can profit from making something of every success, not taking any of them for granted. This is a tough world. We need to be appreciated, and our children do, too.

Afraid you'll make them sinfully full of pride? Forget it. The critical world will keep that knocked out of them. We can counteract discouragement by letting our youngster know that we are proud of him, pleased with what he has accomplished. And we don't have to wait for perfection before we begin to praise him.

Suppose our child brings home a report card with Fs in five subjects and C in one. We can focus on the C for once. It won't really kill us. So what if the C is in sports, something he enjoys, something where there's no homework? We can let him know that we share his enjoyment. We can be glad he's good in sports.

When we begin dishing out praise and acceptance, rewarding our child for whatever we can, his own image of himself will be improved, and success will come more often—in school and out of it.

People often ask me what I think about public schools in comparison with Christian private schools.

I have no quarrel with Christian grade schools or junior highs, but I don't think we need to raise a bunch of hothouse plants, either. I am grateful for the public school training I received when I was a youngster. It gave me a foundation which enables me to stand today and not fall apart with shock at the ways of the world. It didn't shelter me from trouble—it equipped me to cope with it.

I am grateful, too, for Christian schools where spiritual values are taught along with the academics. But we can't bring up our children to avoid the world forever. We have to teach them to live in it.

8

Your Kids and God

When I was eight, I used to hold church services periodically in our basement. I was the preacher, and my brother Bob was the drunk. At every service he'd stagger in, get saved, and sober up.

Ours was not a closed congregation, and we used to invite all the neighbor kids to attend. One of my girl friends had an alcoholic father, and her mother behaved like a professional prostitute. The girl friend and her brother used to come to our "play church" and take turns collecting the offering, ushering people to their chairs, and passing pretend communion.

One day after I had preached one of my sermons on John 3:16, these two kids responded to the altar call. It wasn't

"play church" for them *or* for me that day. They came
forward and really met the Lord Jesus Christ and accepted
Him as their Savior. After that, they began to come to the
"real church" on Sunday, and today that boy is in the ministry.

That early experience was the first of many that persuaded me that church attendance is of vital importance for
us all.

A family brought their youngsters to our teen choir a few
years ago, and the kids just sat there and glared. They didn't
want to attend the church, much less be an active part of the
choir. How they hated it—and me! Week after week they sat
and glowered at me, especially when the Lord would move
me to say something that sounded a little bit spiritual.

One day the kids' mother asked me, "Do you think we're
doing right?"

In the natural, everything in me wanted to give up.

"No, it isn't working," I wanted to say. "Why don't you
take your kids out?" But I resisted the temptation to do that.

"Yes, you're doing the right thing," I assured the mother.
"You're doing what the Word says, and God will honor it.
You're doing the best thing you can do."

The kids were still so hostile, I was almost sorry she took
my advice. But about two weeks later, one glorious night,
one of the boys met the Lord, and another glorious night,
the other one gave his heart to Jesus. Those kids are serving
the Lord today.

I have a friend who has opened her home to unwed
mothers. It is an unwritten law that when girls come to live
with her, they will automatically attend church services
regularly. The rule is easy to enforce, because none of the
girls wants to stay in the house alone while the others go to
church. So far, every young girl who has lived in my friend's

home has gone to church and met the Lord Jesus Christ and had her life totally transformed by Him.

Every child needs the companionship of other people. Every adult needs it too. I've encountered many lonely youngsters. Sometimes they're from large families, but they're still lonely. They have a desire for company, a need to belong. You can teach your youngster that he belongs to daddy and mamma, to his brothers and sisters, and to the family of God. You can satisfy much of the need to belong in your children by teaching them that everyone in the church is part of their family.

A man came into our church service some time ago and met the Lord Jesus Christ for the first time. When he stood to say he was thankful, he began to weep. Everyone sat waiting for him to regain his composure, and finally he was able to speak.

"I never belonged to anyone before in my whole life," he said, "and now I have a family." His outstretched arms embraced the love of the whole congregation.

We take our membership in the family of God so for granted sometimes that we presume that our youngsters feel as we do and know that they belong. They don't always, because too often we have taught them the responsibilities of church membership without saying much about its privileges. We've hammered it into them: "In church you don't do this, and you can't do that, and you have to listen to your Sunday school teacher, and have to go to choir, and have to do a million other things because God wants you to do them."

It's time we gave our kids more positives than negatives about church attendance. We can tell them in so many words, "The people in this church love you. They pray for you. They're your brothers and sisters in Christ, and you belong in the family."

When parents ask me if they should make their kids go to church, I always say yes. When kids are in church, even under duress, they are in a good place for God to become a living part of their lives.

In many cases, kids protest so vociferously over being made to attend church that their parents back down.

"Okay, *make* me go to church," such kids threaten when they see they can't get out of it any other way. "*Make* me go. But after I get away from home, I'll never step inside another church as long as I live!"

Some parents are stampeded by such threats. They chicken out, saying, "Well, honey, if you don't *want* to go—" and they let the kids sleep in on Sunday mornings.

Kids are not able to decide wisely for themselves before they have any real basis on which to make decisions. "It is not in man to do right," the Scripture says, and our own experience bears this out, time after time. Can you handle your life without God? I've tried, and I can't handle mine without Him. On my own, I make a total mess of things. If we know we can't run our own lives without God's help, we should know that our children cannot run theirs by themselves.

If we leave our youngsters outside the church, where are they going to be touched? How are they going to come into the presence of God? The chances of God getting ahold of them are greatly increased when they are regularly in the midst of a fellowship of believers.

While our children are under our roof, we have not only the right but the responsibility to make them go to church. Later, when they have left home for good, if we don't see them serving God, we can say to Him, "Father, while these kids were in my home, I saw to it that they went to Your house. Now I'm counting on You to honor Your promise that when they are old, they will not depart from the upbringing I have given them." He'll hear us. God likes to be reminded of His promises.

But it isn't enough to see to it that our child attends church regularly. The church doesn't have a child enough hours of the week to counteract the whole impact of what the world is feeding him the rest of the time. Parents have to get involved, too, in teaching the things of God to their children.

In God's word, we are told to diligently rehearse in the ears of our children the statutes and laws of God. We are to teach our children to read the Bible and to pray. We are to lead them to become Jesus-centered persons. Where this is not done, the result is often a troubled home, a home where there is no spirituality, no awareness of the presence of Christ.

"But whose responsibility is it?" women sometimes ask me, wanting to point a finger of blame at their husbands.

"It's everybody's responsibility," I tell them. "And what that means is that if your husband won't take the responsibility, it's up to you."

Some women cop out, saying, "But I feel it's my husband's place to take the lead in these things. And my husband isn't interested in spiritual things yet, so I'm just praying and waiting for him to get saved. Then he can step forth as the spiritual leader in our home. I don't want to usurp his place."

In the meantime, those mothers are letting their kids grow up without religious training. They are letting the devil usurp God's place in their lives, all the time piously insisting that they are doing the right thing.

But what if the husband doesn't get saved until after the kids have left the nest? There's no way we can go back and make it up to them if they have moved out from under our sheltering wings without knowing the Lord for themselves, without any foundation in faith to enable them to stand under the pressures of life.

God doesn't see an unbelieving unspiritual husband as the spiritual head of a household. He sees the believing wife in that position. And He holds her responsible, because she's the one to whom He has revealed Himself. She's the one who has turned her life over to Him.

"But what if my husband tells me not to pray with the kids, not to read the Bible with them, not to talk to them about God?"

Such an extreme stand would be rare indeed. In such a case, the wife would have to rely on the Lord, trusting Him to give her supernatural guidance and wisdom. The usual resistance in husbands to religious training for their children is based on unconcern or inconvenience, not on any real objection.

The Bible tells us that the unbelieving husband is sanctified by the believing wife, else were the children unclean, unholy, but now they are clean (I Cor. 7:14). That *can't* mean that the believing wife is supposed to stand by and watch her children grow up without a knowledge of God. She has to bring them up to know the Lord.

The responsibility for seeing to it our youngsters walk with God is one of the most important challenges to parenthood. My boy doesn't have to grow up knowing everything other boys know; my daughter doesn't have to grow up knowing all that other girls know; but God helping me, they will grow up to know all they can of God and His love for them.

This not only means that I should be careful to see that they receive proper Christian training, but also that I should live my life before them in such a way that they can see the importance of priorities in everyday Christian living. American kids have great opportunities for outside activities—everything from tennis lessons to piano instruction—and it's all too easy for such things to push aside more necessary activities—private devotions, spiritual reading, even regular Sunday worship. It's going to be more difficult for my kids to get their own priorities in order if they see me allowing myself to be submerged by outside activities in my own life, to the detriment of the things that I say are necessary to Christian growth.

I'm not saying anything against outside activities. All of them are good—*if* they are seen as secondary to what's lasting. But the Word *has* to come first. The child who knows Jesus *can* make it, no matter what. The child who doesn't know Jesus *can't* make it, no matter what.

One Sunday night, years ago, Danny said to me, "Mom, I want to be baptized in water."

I was in favor of it, of course, but instead of just saying, "That's great!" I asked him, "Why?" I thought he needed to know the answer to that with the clarity that would come from his expressing it verbally for himself.

He thought for just a minute before he answered me. Then he said, "Well, I want to be baptized in water because I'm sorry for my sins, and because I want all the people to know that I'm really going to serve the Lord—and because it's like Jesus dying and coming back alive."

At nine years old, he had grasped something of what Christian baptism is all about.

Children who have been carefully brought up in the nurture of the Lord may still come to a time in their lives when they want to test their faith for themselves.

A Spirit-filled Christian woman told me that her teenage daughters had come to the place where they were really questioning a lot of things.

"Yes, mom, we've always believed this and this," they said, "but it's because that's what you and dad have taught us. But what if Buddhism is right? What if reincarnation is right? What if this is right? Or that?"

"I almost died from shock," the woman said. "We had brought them up to serve the Lord, and now, all of a sudden, they wanted to check it out." But even in the midst of her distress, the woman had uncommon wisdom.

"I held in my feelings," she said. "I told them, 'Yes, you'll have to find out for yourselves that Jesus Christ is alive and that the power of the Holy Spirit is a reality. I can understand that it isn't enough for you just to take my word for it.' "

In her wisdom, she helped the girls come through the period of testing, because she wasn't afraid that her God was too little to make Himself known to them. She wasn't afraid that Christ would let them down. Intuitively, she realized that until they proved Him for themselves, they would never be satisfied, and their faith would not have the foundation that could stand against the storms of life.

Young people often ask themselves, "Is it really that great just being a Christian? It looks like people out in the world have so much fun. Do they really?" Once they have sought the answer for themselves and God Himself has satisfied them, they're on the rock.

A teenager is at the point of life where he is testing everything he's been taught to see whether or not it will really work. Sometimes parents interpret as rebellion what is merely a teenager's checking out of the practicality of what he's been taught. What works, he keeps. What doesn't work, he's better off without, and so he throws it away. If your own teenagers are going through a phase where they suddenly seem to be against all you've taught them, relax. It's temporary. Thank God that they're testing things for themselves. If you've done your job properly, training them up in the way they should go, they'll seek the truth and find it.

The likelihood that our youngsters may come to such a time of testing for themselves is one reason why we need to be careful what we teach them about God. Only what is true can stand during a time of testing. What is false will be shown for what it is.

In this, as in other areas of rearing our children, we teach through far more than our deliberately spoken words of instruction on the subject. We teach our children about God by our own example of right living, by our attitudes toward Him, and by our own relationship to Jesus as it is evidenced in our worship of Him.

When I was a child, I had the frightening experience of hearing the chorus, "Watching you, watching you, there's an all-seeing eye watching you. . . ." For years, all across the sky, I saw a horrible eyeball, always focused on me. I didn't like it. Nobody likes to be watched all the time. Over the years, somebody had to work extra hard at teaching me "God is love," to overcome that uneasiness.

Years ago, when I was working with the courts in probation, I went into a home where there was a picture of God hanging over the table. When the youngsters complained about the food on their plates, the mother pointed to the picture and threatened to tell God on them. I became so upset, so angry, thinking how that kind of teaching could damage a child's relationship to God that I had to withdraw from the case and send someone else to handle it.

There are so many ways that parents are tempted to "use" God in training children. Once my brother Bob couldn't find out which of his daughters had done a certain prohibited thing. The girls, who were about thirteen and fourteen at the time, conspired together and agreed that they wouldn't tell him.

"You'll just have to lick us both," they challenged him, sure that he would back down at such a prospect. But Bob said, "That's all right. You don't have to say a word. The Lord will tell me who did it. I'm going to ask Him."

Bob went into his room to pray for a while, and when he came back out, he said, "Lynette, the Lord told me it was you."

"Well," she said, "if the Lord told you I did it, then I guess you had better lick me." Years later, he learned that Judy had been the culprit, not Lynette. But Lynette had taken the licking.

The girls had no feeling that God was not omniscient in this case, but they were certain that dad wasn't as smart as he thought. The point is that we must never "use" God in our relationships with our children.

Prayer is a natural thing for a child. Sometimes parents who have turned away from God themselves learn to their surprise that their children have quite a regular habit of prayer. Somewhere they picked up the idea that they could talk to God, and all by themselves, they began to do it.

I remember reading about the day when Helen Keller's teacher wanted to tell her about God. She began by spelling the word "God" into Helen's hand, and then she spelled more words to explain that God made the whole world and sent His Son, Jesus, to die for us. Helen's face lit up, and she spelled some words back into her teacher's hand: "Oh! God has spoken to me many times. I'm so glad you told me His name."

One day my Danny said, "Well, mom, I know the Lord isn't going to come until my friend Joe is saved."

"Praise the Lord," I said, "but why isn't Joe saved already?"

"I'm not sure, mom," he acknowledged, "but I think it's because Jesus is trying my patience to see if I'll keep on praying."

If our youngster reaches a point where he doesn't want to say his prayers, we don't have to crowd him about it. We can accept it matter-of-factly, and say his prayers for him:

"Dear Jesus, Robert comes to You tonight, but he's too tired to say his own prayers, so I'm saying them for him. Robert loves You, Jesus. . . ."

If we don't make an issue of it, the child will return to saying his own prayers before long. One mother told me of a prayer experience with her seven-year-old. Every night after the mother had read her child a Bible story or two, the child would say, "You say my prayers for me, mamma. I'm too shy to pray out loud."

The mother didn't crowd her, just said the prayers while the child snuggled under the covers. Sometimes after the mother had said, "Amen," Ruthie would remind her, "Mamma, you forgot to tell Jesus about my sore toe," or whatever it was, and so mamma would pray a little bit more.

There came a day when Ruthie said, "Mamma, tonight I wanna say my prayers myself." And she did—probably the fastest, most staccato prayer in all of Christendom. And the glory of the Lord fell down all over the place. As the mother was turning out the light to go downstairs, Ruthie said, "Mamma, at Sunday school my teacher says that if I won't pray out loud with the rest of the kids, I have to stand outside in the hallway."

The mystery of why Ruthie hadn't been able to pray her own prayers was solved. Someone's attempt to force her to pray had pushed her away from prayer. Her mother's loving acceptance had brought her back. It's not by forcing but by faithfulness that parents help their children toward a closer relationship with God.

It is good for our children to know that nothing is beneath God's attention. Again, they learn a lot by our example.

Once Debbie's dog got sick. For two days, she had moped around, and we didn't know what to do for her. I knew that Debbie was worried, and I finally prayed about the situation.

"This sounds dumb, Lord," I said, "but I need You to help me know what's wrong with Babette."

Almost before I could finish my prayer and say amen, I heard myself saying, "I'm going to take the dog to the vet to be wormed."

The vet confirmed the Lord's diagnosis. Babette had worms.

"Mom, how did you know that?" Debbie asked me after we got home.

"You aren't going to believe this," I told her, "but I got on my knees before God about the dog and He let me know what the trouble was. Honest."

Debbie did believe it, and we both had a good lesson in prayer that day—that God cares about every little thing we give to Him.

If we can create the right kind of climate for our child to learn to take everything to God in prayer while he is still a grade-schooler, we'll have a powerful ally on our side and

God's side for the child's adolescent years.

One mother told me about her teenage daughter who was about to drive the whole family up the wall with her negative attitude toward helping out with household chores. She did the bare minimum of what was required of her, but reluctantly. Her general approach was so complaining, so down at the mouth, it was making life miserable for everyone. The mother ignored it as long as she could, and then finally, when the situation didn't improve but seemed to worsen with the passing weeks, she had to say something.

"Julie," she said, as gently as she could, "you have been acting so unhappy about doing your share of the work this summer. I don't think I've been requiring any more of you than I have of the other kids, and I'm at a complete loss to know what's wrong."

Julie was frowning when the mother began her little speech, and she was frowning even harder in the midst of it. Asked if she had an explanation, Julie offered tight-lipped sullen silence.

"Tell you what I'd like you to do for me, Julie," her mother said. "I'd like for you to pray and seek God's will in all this." There was no scolding, no harangue, no condemnation, just the mother's invitation for the daughter to take the matters at issue up with the highest possible authority.

"I noticed a change in her almost immediately," the mother told me. "By the next morning, it was obvious to all of us that something wonderful had happened. Julie was doing her work cheerfully, just like in the good old days, even volunteering to do some things that were not strictly required of her. After a few days, I just had to thank her for being so helpful."

"Oh, mamma," Julie told her, "I did what you said. I prayed about my attitude, and—" Tears filled her eyes as she went on, "I just wish there was some way I could make up to you for how ugly I've been all summer—"

To the mother, all the ugliness was more than atoned for already.

When our teenagers have been brought up to have a living prayer relationship with a God who is real, new creaturehood can set in over and over again.

9

Your Kids and Their Emotions

In dealing with adults, I have found that their problems often stem from a childhood of suppressed emotions. They wanted to say, "I'm mad. I hate. I want to kill." But if they had given verbal expression to such feelings as these, *they'd* have been killed themselves.

Don't tell me that you've never hated. I won't believe you. Don't tell me that you've never had an urge to kill. I know you have. I've been there. If you haven't had those feelings toward someone else, you've had them toward yourself, wishing you could drop dead to get out of something that was unbearable for you.

Kids have the same feelings. And more times than not, when they speak them out, we punish them. By doing that, we teach them to suppress their feelings, to deny even vocal expression to their natural instincts. The result of all this suppression is psychopaths, liars, killers, and people who crack up because they have been denied the normal expression of normal feelings.

Why do we do it? We do it out of pride. We have been taught to control ourselves, not to let our feelings show. And we try to teach our children to do the same thing.

We want to be proud of their behavior, and because we know that the average person might not understand if our child yelled or stomped his foot, we try to keep him from doing it. We don't want anyone to think we have lost control over our kids, and so we make them inhibit the natural expression of their emotions. Too often, we're not teaching control but suppression.

A wise parent will encourage a child to express his feelings verbally instead of requiring him to stifle them.

A friend of mine talked with her son a short time after he'd been involved in a fight with a playmate. She was anxious for him not to feel guilty about the feelings he had.

"I'll bet it really made you mad when Johnny tipped over your tricycle," she said.

"Yeah, it sure did," her son replied. "I wanted to slug him."

"I can understand how you feel," she said. "I've felt that way myself when someone has bothered something of mine."

"You have?"

"Oh, yes. Lots of times."

Her son was surprised to learn that his mother had feelings of anger too. This knowledge made his own feelings more acceptable to him, and he was open to learning from her how to deal with anger and other feelings.

If we are careful *not* to seize every available opening for preaching at our youngsters, they will come to maturity more quickly. By not giving them any advice to resist, we clear the way for them to move forward at a surprisingly rapid rate sometimes.

If the parent had told the child his anger was wrong instead of encouraging him to understand it and work through it, the situation would undoubtedly have become worse as the child added his bottled-up frustration to his initial, natural, response of anger and guilt.

Kids from age six on need to understand what happens in their systems when they become angry. They don't have to know the word adrenalin, but they can understand that some chemical is released inside their bodies when they become angry. When that happens, they automatically want to fight. And they're stronger when they're angry—because of all that adrenalin.

Simply to tell a child that anger and fighting are wrong won't change how he feels. The next time the adrenalin pours through his system, he's going to want to hit somebody, just as he did before we explained it to him. But we can help him act acceptably if we tell him, "Yes, the chemical that comes into your bloodstream when you are angry has to be gotten rid of somehow, but you don't have to hit anybody. Instead, you can let it help you run fast as lightning around the block."

Our youngster will probably find this an intriguing thing, and the next time he gets mad, he might leave his tormentor standing mystified on the sidewalk while he races around the block just to see how much faster he can go with the extra chemical helping him out.

It is important to help a child understand what goes on inside him, to give him tangible reasons for his feelings so he won't develop the notion in his mind, "I'm just no good."

In actuality, we think it's worse for our child to hit a person than to speak evil of him. And yet, in the idealism of parenthood, we make the mistake of teaching our kids that one is as bad as the other because the Lord said that thinking the wrong thing is the same as doing it.

We're going to have trouble if we teach that to our children. If we say to our youngster, "Johnny, it's just as wrong for you to say it as to do it," he may go out and clobber the first kid who crosses him. Society places a greater penalty on the actual striking than on the threatening words, and our children have to learn this so they can govern themselves accordingly. When they're old enough to understand—and the age of understanding varies greatly from one child to another—we can deal with the attitudes behind wrong actions, but behavior patterns have to come into line before then.

Danny's fast fists had resulted in bloodied noses and irate mothers a number of times before it occurred to me to train him to do something to prevent such undesirable results of anger.

"The first thing to do when you feel yourself getting mad is to put your hands in your pockets," I told him. "And keep them there."

The idea sounded so kooky, he was willing to try it. I'd look out the window and see a very red-faced little boy, his hands shoved ferociously down in his pockets, and breathe a sigh of relief that he was learning to control his temper.

We can actually use our child's emotional outbursts to strengthen family relationships. There's nothing more binding in love than to join another person in an emotion. When our youngster is full of hate, we can tell him we understand it. If he hates flies, we hate flies with him. If he hates birds, we don't preach to him about how beautiful birds are, and how God made them for us to enjoy. We agree with him that our windshield is really ugly when it's all splattered with droppings from the sparrows in the trees. We confess that we didn't like it when the crows plucked up the corn in our garden about as soon as it sprouted.

When our child says he hates people, if we say, "Oh, honey, you mustn't hate people," we haven't taken his hate away. We may have intensified it by making him think it's not okay for him to express his feelings verbally. As a result, he resolves to bury his feelings from now on, and later we have to pay a psychiatrist fifty dollars an hour to dig them up again.

Instead of trying to stifle his animosities when someone has done something he doesn't like, we can try to get him to put himself in the other person's place, to examine the other person's motivation.

"Why do you think he did it?" we can ask our child. Thinking through, our child may learn a lot.

When a child is frustrated because he has lost something vital, I don't know of a better thing to do than to join him in his frustration. It's not the time to lecture him, "Well, I've told you that if you continued to be so careless about your things, keeping your room in such a mess, that someday you'd lose something very important to you—"

When our youngster is upset already, we don't want to add guilt to his burden, to be an I-told-you-so. That's not what he needs. If we give him moral support, he'll do his own judging of himself. That will result in changed behavior patterns eventually, whereas our preaching will result only in resistance to change.

We can be as sympathetic as possible with our frustrated child, without being overly wordy about it. Saying something simple is helpful, something like, "I know just how you feel, Johnny. It really bugs me to lose something."

We can join the search for the lost item. We can even express his outrage for him:

"It's gotta be around here somewhere. We're going to find that stupid thing if it takes all night!"

The effect on him of our sputterings will be instant calming. If we're going to do the fuming and fussing for him, he doesn't have to work up such a sweat himself. It can even get kind of funny, and laughter is one of the best ways to clear the atmosphere of frustration. Once the loser begins to relax in his attitude toward the lost thing, his mind might clear enough to remember where it is. If that doesn't happen, we can join him in praying that God will show him where the misplaced item is hiding.

Trying to deal with frustration by a frontal assault on the child's carelessness is like trying to dip ice cream while it's frozen hard as a brick. We'll just break the tool without getting the job accomplished.

Some youngsters are extremely sensitive in their emotional makeup. A wise parent will not try to stamp out sensitivity, but will encourage it, directing it into the right channels. When a youngster is embroiled in conflict because of his sensitivity, we can explain, "That's how it is. Anytime you get really involved with life, someone may be unhappy. But how awful it would be *not* to feel for the hurts of other people. We'd be like zombies, then."

We can let our sensitive youngster know that there will always be kids who will hate his guts because he champions the underdog instead of joining in the attack. No one who stirs up trouble will love the peacemaker. We can explain to our child that there is a price to be paid for any kind of involvement—on the right side or the wrong one.

"But I'm proud of you for standing up for what's right," we can tell him. And he'll have a healthy attitude about his own right standing, too.

One Sunday night in our church, a challenge to the youth was given. When the invitation hymn was sung, many young people began coming forward to "give their all" to the Lord. I noticed that my daughter was not among them. She just kept sitting in her seat, and I wondered about it. My natural instinct after the meeting was to ask her why she hadn't gone to the altar, but I had learned not to do this. I got at it in an underhanded kind of way, thinking I could get by with it.

"I tell you," I said to her, "it really thrilled me to see those young people giving their all to the Lord."

I was trying to be clever, subtle, trying to get around the rules, but almost immediately I sensed that I had exerted too much pressure. I had to undo the damage I'd done.

I've learned that humor can be a good tool in situations where I've royally goofed it, and so I turned to her and asked in a very joking tone, "Debbie, did you give your all to Jesus?"

"You saw me sitting there in my seat, didn't you?" she asked. "I didn't come to the altar, did I?"

"But what does that tell me?" I went on.

"Well, it probably tells you that I didn't give my all, doesn't it, mom?"

I sensed a little sparking of a joke coming from her then, and I could see I hadn't ruined our relationship by my mistake.

"No ma'am, it doesn't," I said. "There could have been another reason why you didn't come forward—"

Her voice was all seriousness then, but happy, as she

explained, "I wanted to go forward with the rest, mom, but my skirt was too wrinkled."

I was grateful that God had prevented me from blowing that one completely. What I could well have read as stubbornness, a tinge of rebellion, and reinforced in my unwisdom, was just sensitivity. Debbie was embarrassed about her wrinkled skirt. It would have looked bad if she had walked forward.

We can learn to recognize and reward sensitivity in our children by being sensitive ourselves to what the situation really is or could be.

Boredom is another feeling frequently manifested in the lives of our children. How can we cope with boredom in them? What can we do when they complain, "There's nothing to do around here"?

The imaginative parent can cope with boredom in children in a variety of ways. One of the simplest is to give them something to do that will exercise their imaginations. Modeling clay or paper and paste are favorites for them to work with. Don't worry about the mess they will make; find something for them to do that will exercise their imagination or stimulate their own initiative.

I remember one year when a friend and I had three of our kids housebound with illness during a big snow. They were bored to death with their inactivity, and the snow was too beautiful to waste, so we bundled the kids up, plunked them on the back porch, and carried buckets of snow up to them so they could make their own miniature snowmen.

The adventure didn't give them a relapse. The unexpected fun probably made them get well quicker.

One of the things that causes boredom is too much of the same old routine day after day, too much predictability in life. If a child thinks he knows everything that is going to happen every day of the week, naturally he'll be bored to death. Parents need to be alert to liven up life a little for kids who are reflecting the blah attitude, "Life is one long, dull, meaningless rut. Nothing interesting ever happens around here. What's the use of living?"

We can plan something unexpected. We can give our youngsters the thrill of surprises more often than just on Christmas or birthdays.

My mother had a real knack for making surprises. From time to time, in spite of the busyness of her life as a mother of five kids and helper of my dad in his ministry, we kids would come home from school to find the dining room table elegantly set with tablecloth, candles, flowers—the whole works.

"Who's coming?" we'd ask her.

"Nobody," she'd say. "I just thought it would be nice to eat in the dining room instead of in the kitchen, for a change." Soft music would be coming from the radio, and the air would be full of the aroma of something wonderful in the oven. It was probably just meat loaf and potatoes, but everybody got all cleaned up to eat it. The boys would slick their hair back just as if it was Sunday.

Occasionally, we were permitted to take a plate of food and go sit by the fireplace—just for something different. We can try something like that if we are in a rut of routine in our household; we can break out of our self-made mold. The whole world won't crumble if we change the usual for the unusual once in a while.

Some time ago, I threw a bomb into the center of my living room by walking in and turning off the television set. A shocking thing to do in our day and age! Both my kids went into orbit.

"Hey, mom! What's wrong with you? We want to see that program!"

"Nothing's wrong with me," I announced. "But no TV tonight. We're going to play together, instead, for a change."

Well, the first half hour, there was a little pouting, but it wasn't long before the three of us were having a hilariously good time competing in a game. What I did took a lot of nerve. Who was I to think I could compete with TV? But it worked.

If everything we suggest as a boredom-fighting recreational activity meets with negative response, we can assign the child a specific job to do. The job should be difficult enough to require him to stretch his maturity level a little. We can ask him to make a cake for supper, concoct a pizza, bake a couple of loaves of bread. Those are creative and useful activities for a boy or a girl. The child will probably greet the assignment with grumbling, but if we insist that he do it, he's likely to get interested in spite of himself.

If we are free to work *with* our child, a boring, nothing-to-do afternoon is a perfect time to excavate his closet or his dresser drawers. We might even get him to help us clean out the garage or the attic, or paint the laundry room. Doing something we can do together, when possible, converts draggy boredom time into priceless togetherness time.

Teenagers are not children; they're not adults. They are in the midst of rapid change, and it's not all uphill. They vacillate from one moment to the next. They can respond to us as an adult, and we can react to them as to an adult. In the twinkling of an eye, they may revert back to childhood. About the time we've readjusted to that level, they've switched back, and we're wrong again.

Their emotions can go from one extreme to another in nothing flat. Naturally frustrating to the parent or social worker or teacher, this can be even more frustrating to the teenager himself. But it's all part of living, part of growing up. And if we have learned to love our children, we'll survive their roller coaster ups and downs—knowing that they'll emerge as mature, stable adults in the fullness of time.

10

Your Kids and Sex

The area of physical and sexual relationships seems to be one of the most difficult for parents to handle, and it is, at the same time, one of the most important ones for us to handle properly.

At first glance, it would seem that our responsibility could be broken down into two main areas: providing sound information and training right attitudes. Actually, however, the two are so closely interrelated, it is difficult, if not impossible, to separate one from the other. This is good. It means that we have an opportunity to teach our children right attitudes along with every bit of information we impart to them.

Our bodies are wonderfully made, and answering kids' questions about them is one of the greatest privileges of parenthood. With every question our child asks us, he hands us an opportunity to guide his life.

"When should I begin to tell my child where babies come from?" is a question parents often ask. No one can set down a hard and fast age limit, because children are not all cut from the same pattern. Some have an earlier curiosity than others. As a general rule, when a child is old enough to ask a question, he is old enough to handle the answer to it. Certainly we should never turn aside our youngster's questions about the origin of life, because if we don't answer his questions for him, someone else will, someone who may instill wrong attitudes in the process.

In attempting to answer children's questions, we need to be sure that we have really heard and understood what they're asking. Only then can we be sure we are making an appropriate reply. For instance, a child's "Mamma, where did Uncle Harry come from?" is likely to require a simple, "From Atlanta," instead of a lengthy birds and bees explanation.

From preschool on, youngsters have some awareness of their sexuality. Between sixty and seventy percent of boys under nine years of age have had a sexual experience of some kind with themselves. The little baby face look is no excuse for not teaching a youngster anything about his sex drives.

"But I'm too reticent and shy to talk about sex with my kids," you say? Instead of being proud of our reticence, we should strive to put aside our embarrassment and shyness and learn to talk with our youngsters about the things that concern them.

If we absolutely cannot make ourselves uninhibited enough to respond to our child's needs in this area, we can give him answers indirectly. Public libraries, church libraries, and religious bookstores have many beautiful and sound sex education books written from a wholesome Christian perspective. We can examine some books on these subjects, and buy or borrow the ones with which we feel most comfortable.*

If we're smart, we'll acquire these aids *before* our child comes to us with the loaded questions. We may be surprised at how easy it is to sit down with our questioning youngster and read through the books with him. Hopefully, we'll find our own inhibitions relaxing as we read about how wonderfully God has planned for Christian marriage to provide loving families for new babies born into the world. We may gain a new respect for our bodies and be educated along with our child.

From the ages of two to five, youngsters are quite naturally interested in reproduction, particularly if there's a new baby on the way. There's no need to turn their curiosity aside if there's a pregnancy in our family. We can make it beautiful and precious to them.

My Debbie was five when Danny was born. She had a good time putting her hand on my abdomen while we counted the unborn baby's kicks together. We talked about whether it would be a boy or girl. She helped me pick out a name for the baby. Sometimes, I must admit, she asked me some rather embarrassing questions. But they shouldn't have been embarrassing to me. A child's curiosity is not embarrassed. It is natural, normal, wholesome, and it needs to be satisfied.

If an otherwise normal child has not asked us any questions about his sexuality by the time he is twelve years old, we need to initiate some discussions on the subject. Again,

---

* For a list of suggested books, see Appendix.

well-planned books can be a big help in breaking the ice, in overcoming barriers of false modesty or embarrassment.

Perhaps our youngster has already entered his teens and we are certain that he has received certain basic sex information from his peers or his teachers, but the two of us have never discussed anything in this area. There's no justification for putting it off any longer. Our child needs to feel that he can come to us with his questions and problems in this area of his life. If the right opportunity doesn't seem to present itself, we can create an opportunity on our own. The same libraries and bookstores that have helpful sex education books for smaller children have many soundly written books for teens, giving Bible-based answers to the questions they might ask.

We don't have to sit down and read these books *with* our teenager, of course, but we should read them before we hand them to him. We can say, "Here's something I found in the bookstore the other day that might be interesting to you." If that direct approach is too tough for us, we could leave a good book or two on our teen's dresser or desk where he's sure to see it. We can add new books to his collection from time to time, doing all we can to open a channel of communication.

In raising boys, we need to help them understand what happens to their bodies at puberty, so they won't be afraid or ashamed. They need to know why they feel how they feel, and what they're supposed to do with their feelings. They need to be taught how to control their drives. This very essential instruction has to be given at home, where emotional training can be combined with sexual training.

Problems with masturbation sometimes arise in teenagers who develop psychological problems due to inadequate or improper teaching. Some boys grow up thinking they are different from everyone else, condemned by God and condemned by society if people found out about them.

If youngsters are to grow up with a satisfactory sexual adjustment to life, they must be taught to understand themselves and their sexuality. If little boys could know they're going to have certain feelings, certain dreams, and if little girls were taught that they might be physically aroused by some little boy's remark, they would have fewer problems in handling what life brings to them.

When our little girl questions us about her normal, biological reaction to something a boy has said to her, we don't have to squelch her with an outraged, "That was a naughty little boy to talk to you that way! I don't want you to speak to him again as long as you live!" That would set up in the girl's mind a dangerous rejection of her sexuality. She'd begin to feel that sex is a dirty word, a no-no.

When we find our youngsters handling their own genitals, we don't have to rant and rave and carry on, saying, "That's terrible!" or "Jesus doesn't like that!" If we do, we plant seeds of guilt, and later on, when our daughters are supposed to have a beautiful honeymoon with the man of their dreams, their subconscious may prevent it. A better way to handle such a situation is simply to say matter-of-factly, "It would be better if you didn't do that." Give them something else to occupy their attention. It doesn't have to be an issue, and we don't have to be psychologists to handle it.

An attractive young married woman came to me for counseling recently. She claimed to be in love with her husband, but she confessed, "I just can't stand for him to touch me in any intimate way. Our sexual relations are pure agony for me—"

As she told me about her life, going way back to her

childhood, we found the root of her problem. When she was four years old, her mother had found her with a little boy in a barn. She had her panties pulled down and the little boy was standing there, looking at her. The mother was furious. She spanked the little girl hard then and there, shamed her with loud indignation, marched her into the house without her panties, and made her stand before the whole family and tell them what she had done. Then the mother went to the little boy's house and made the child go through the same nightmarish scene with them.

The child herself didn't realize how scarred she was from the experience until she grew up and got married. She had assumed that it would be natural for her to make a normal sexual adjustment to marriage, but her life was hell. After she realized where her frigidity had begun, she was able to receive forgiveness and let the inhibiting scar tissue be done away with.

There is no need to overreact when we catch small youngsters looking at each other's external sex organs. This is common, the result of a natural curiosity. It is not necessarily or automatically naughtiness.

When parents discover youngsters looking at one another in this way, they sometimes make loud noises of disgust and move in immediately to separate the youngsters. A harsh scolding follows, often accompanied by a severe spanking, and a guilt-producing, "I don't want you to play with Johnny ever again—he's a nasty boy!"

Maybe the incident wasn't Johnny's fault. Our own pink and precious little darling Lucinda might have suggested the new game.

No matter who was at fault, we can't afford to set the stage for the child to think that sex is evil.

We can approach the youngsters calmly, and speak to our

own child loud enough for the others to hear, but without condemning angry language. A simple, "I don't want you to do that any more," is adequate. An acceptable activity can be suggested for everybody. After that, of course, we will want to supervise our child's playtime more closely for a while. We can provide the setting for happy, acceptable recreation, and do away with the temptation of garages or other concealed play areas by putting locks on doors or otherwise making them effectively out-of-bounds.

It is not necessary for parents to be forever spying on their children, but we shouldn't wear blinders, either. We should trust our children as far as we reasonably can. If we find evidence of forbidden behavior a second time, we should handle it as calmly as we did at first. If the misbehavior persists, we can employ some form of punishment that will dissuade future action along the same lines. It is important to make clear to the child that the spanking or the withdrawal of privileges is not because the thing he did was so wrong in itself, but because he had been disobedient to our rules.

Unlike many Christian parents, I'm pleased that schools are getting involved in the area of sex education. That in no way lessens parental responsibility, but as the kids bring books and information home from school, a door is opened that can help us to relax our hangups so we *can* talk about such things. Parents who are already doing their job at home can feel confident that their kids won't be led astray by what the teacher says at school. And parents who haven't done anything at home are sometimes challenged to begin, in order to counteract what they feel is wrong teaching at school.

A nineteen-year-old girl came to me recently, saying, "Iverna, so help me God, my parents are Christians, but I have never discussed menstruating or sex with either one of them in my whole life. Two people have taught me every-thing I know—a girlfriend and a boy who almost got me in trouble."

In our country, with all its looseness and immorality, we still have young people entering marriage with only the sketchiest information about sexual relationships. They are discovering by the action what sex is about. A good program of sex education in the schools can help to correct that situation. But the schools cannot take the place of parents in teaching the right attitudes toward sexual relationships. Parents do not always realize this. They may turn away from the God-given responsibility for training their children be-cause the kids have more formal education than the parents.

One day I was speaking with the father of a teenage boy who knew very little about sex and yet whose drives were at their peak. The boy was behaving in some ways that were socially unacceptable, and his mother had asked me to persuade the boy's father to talk to him.

"Me? Talk to my kid about sex?" the father blurted out at me. "Why, my son knows a lot more about sex than I do."

The son, who had gotten his limited information about sex from school and friends, couldn't possibly know more than the father did, unless he'd had more experience. Biological plumbing diagrams on the blackboard in a hygiene class do not constitute adequate knowledge about sex for a sixteen-year-old. What he had learned from his peers was equally inadequate for his real needs. Kids had probably told him little more than, "Sex is the neatest thing that ever happened to anybody. The establishment says it's a no-no, so that automatically makes it a yes-yes. Man, you oughtta try it!"

"Trying it" in the back seat of somebody's car, scared to death he'd get caught, would increase his need to learn what his father could teach him in the area of attitudes.

When parents assume their kids know all there is to know, they make a big mistake.

"Well, my goodness," one heartbroken mother said to me, "my daughter's been dating since she was thirteen. She should have known the score."

Another shook her head and said, "I just can't understand what's gotten into him. My son never gave us any trouble at all before this happened."

Where parents have neglected their responsibility to talk to their children about these matters, it's no wonder that so many eighteen-year-old kids are all mixed up. A boy goes to a counselor and says, "This probably sounds silly, but I don't know how I'm *supposed* to act on a date."

Or a fellow will hang his head in embarrassment while I make a few preliminary remarks, kind of to break the ice, and then he'll look straight at me and blurt out, "I think I'm oversexed."

A little nonjudgmental questioning usually reveals that he's a perfectly normal male.

Sometimes a girl comes in and says, "I'm afraid there must be something wrong with me. Every guy I go out with—"

She sheds a few tears as she describes their behavior. Such distress could be avoided if mothers would teach their daughters not to do certain things that are practically guaranteed to turn a guy on.

Some girls, even Christian girls, dress in such come-hither clothes and behave in such "Take me, baby, I'm yours" ways that I can understand why fellows get them in trouble. The girls ask for it—and yet probably do it in all innocence, being ignorant of the biological makeup of boys.

Another reason we have so many unwed mothers today is because of the lack of proper teaching of our sons. Many parents have put all the emphasis on teaching their daughters to be chaste and clean, in teaching them how to behave on a date and how not to, and they've let the boys grow up just any old way. But girls don't impregnate girls.

Many boys have the attitude that they are entitled to take any girl they can get, because they saw their mothers as servants of all instead of as partners with their fathers, queens in loving relationships with kings in their homes. If father belittled mother, he was inadvertently teaching his son, "Women are to be looked down upon." If mother said to the child, "Don't talk to me that way," and dad heard but didn't follow up, the boy learned from dad's silence that women could be treated with contempt. How in the world can such a boy be expected to respect the girls he dates and the woman he marries?

Discrimination in the assignment of household chores is another factor contributing to the lack of respect some boys have for girls. Sometimes girls are taught to cook and sew, to iron, fold clothes, and wash dishes, but because there isn't much wood-splitting or yard work to be done, the boys aren't asked to help. Doing chores is an important part of growing up to responsible maturity. If housework is the only work we have for our boy to do, we should put him to work at it. It won't make a sissy out of him. It will help him learn responsibility, and it will help him learn respect for girls, too.

We must teach our sons that every time they pick up a date at her door, they are responsible under God and to her parents for how they treat her. When they deliver her to her door again, she should feel that she has been treated with respect, that her womanhood has been enhanced rather than degraded. God created men and women to be complements of one another, and our sons' actions should reflect that knowledge.

As parents, we can do a lot toward setting the stage for proper boy-girl dating relationships. We can leave the living room when our daughter is entertaining her date—but not until after we've been with them for a while. Our presence kind of lingers, setting an unseductive atmosphere. We can create a healthy rapport with our youngsters—and their dates—by making them aware of our presence in a friendly way.

Where did we get off on this big they-don't-want-parents-around-so-we're-going-to-leave kick? It doesn't help our kids.

I didn't want my parents hanging around either when my boyfriends came to call, but they were always there anyway, just as big as life.

"Men love darkness," the Bible says, and one blessing of having parents is that they watch out for their kids, to keep them from getting in trouble.

11

A Look behind Misbehavior

In the young child's mind, his parents are a physical part of him, just as his arms and legs are. Understanding this will help us to understand our youngsters' behavior patterns. This is why they care so much that we're away as much as we are, why they are concerned when we're cross, why they pretend they don't care if we ever come home or not. They have to build up defense mechanisms in order to survive without too much pain.

When we are ignorant of these things, we unwittingly put our child in situations where elaborate defenses are necessary for his ego. What looks like misbehavior might be the child's way of trying to communicate, "I hurt."

We're not cross with our youngster when he cries in pain

or when he's physically sick, and yet when he's emotionally disturbed and lashes out, we are likely to call it misbehavior, and punish it by spanking or taking away privileges. But treating the symptom doesn't get at the root of the problem. We need to see what our child's misbehavior is trying to communicate to us.

Maybe our youngster has always been very well-behaved, and all of a sudden he is fighting, being irritable, doing everything he knows is wrong. Many parents fall apart in frustration when this happens and start beating the child, putting him down somehow. But that doesn't help—it makes things worse.

What we need to do is to look at our youngster's world and see if something has changed in it. We need to look at ourselves, too. Have we been away from home more than usual? Has the child's father been more preoccupied with his work than is customary? Have we heard ourselves saying, "Leave daddy alone, he's busy"? Has daddy been saying the same thing about us? If so, what the child has heard is, "Part of you is being denied," and he has reacted to it.

The same kind of reaction is likely to occur when anything else claims attention the child thought was his.

How thrilled we were the first time our child said mamma or daddy, and the first time he used a spoon successfully. Everyone in the family was called in to listen or to watch.

"Go ahead, honey—that's right—put it in your mouth. See that! Isn't that a big boy?"

Everyone clapped. Everyone was tickled to death that the baby was learning to feed himself. He had achieved a new thing.

The first time our child brought papers home from school, we pored over them, oohing and aahing over the beautiful picture even though we couldn't figure out which side was supposed to be up. Everything was a big deal. In the midst of it all, our youngster was basking in acceptance, security, and love.

Then came the day when he brought his arithmetic home after a new baby had arrived and we were up to our ears in diapers, bottles, and sleepless nights. That's when we inadvertently began teaching our child something other than acceptance, security, and love.

"Look, mommy, I learned that two and three make five if they have the right base."

We took an impatient look, mumbled, "Yeah, honey, that's nice. Run along now. Can't you see I'm busy?"

The child was baffled. Where was all the loving attention he had taken for granted all these years? The bottom had fallen out of his world. All of a sudden he felt rejected, insecure, unloved. And we wondered why behavior problems began to erupt in him.

When a youngster misbehaves in order to get attention, we need to recognize that we might not be giving him enough of the right kind of attention. Giving a child plenty of the right kind of attention *before* he asks for it is the ounce of prevention that's worth more than tons of cure.

Infants and preschoolers are more inclined to be friendly than unfriendly unless they've really been hurt, their drives stymied. But when we take our loving little dear who's always been such an agreeable sweetheart, so easy to get along with, to nursery school, there he meets a new thing. Everybody doesn't suddenly melt when he looks up at them with his big blue eyes and says, "I wuv you." Some people tell him to *please* sit down and be quiet. The child's behavior at home will begin to reflect this baffling rejection thing that has come into his life without warning.

Aware of the cause, we know *not* to punish the child and

thereby make the problem worse, but to show him an increased measure of love and acceptance at home. That will help him make a satisfactory adjustment to the school situation.

We can forestall some attention-getting misbehavior by anticipating circumstances where our youngster might be deprived of attention. Making special provision to meet his needs can eliminate the necessity for misbehavior on his part.

Every mother has been in situations where a guest in the home has required her undivided attention. Perhaps she has been involved in extra cleaning, extra cooking, and paying exclusive attention to the guest. The child who is ignored in the midst of such circumstances is likely to become a hellion—forcing attention on himself by spilling his milk, jumping from the coffee table, maybe even by kicking the honored guest in the shins when nobody else is looking.

The mother, embarrassed and frustrated, at a loss to know what to do, does every wrong thing in the book. First, she tells the child again and again to stop the wrong thing he is doing—but she never enforces her instruction. Maybe he is banging his shoe against the table leg. He never stops, but keeps on doing it, figuring he's probably safe from punishment for his disobedience. He *knows* his mother won't spank him with company present. Meanwhile, he's the center of attention and having a ball. As long as he continues to bang his shoe, someone will be glowering at him. Unfavorable attention is better than none, he thinks.

The next mistake the mother makes is to talk about his misbehavior in his presence, magnifying it, increasing the sought-after attention that is the cause of it.

"I don't know what's gotten into Mark today," she apologizes to the guest who is contemplating the run in her brand-new panty hose. Underneath the run, her leg is beginning to turn black and blue from precious little Mark's shenanigans.

"I've never seen him this naughty before," the mother goes on, her eyes dangerously off Mark for an instant—just long enough for him to deliberately sling his arm against the centerpiece on the table and send it crashing and splashing. Something in him insists that he live up to the character that's being painted.

A piece of the flying glassware hits his mother on the shin and makes a run in *her* brand-new panty hose.

The jig is up.

Mother sputters something mercifully not understandable, swoops the child up, carries him as far out of earshot as possible, and whips him until her arm aches. He screams, she seethes and dumps him in bed, totally rejected. Gritting her teeth, she throws him a look of utter contempt, closes the door softly, glues a fake smile on her flushed face, and goes back downstairs to entertain her guest.

But the guest is gone.

There's a note on the table beside the pieces of broken glass the thoughtful guest had picked out of the carpet.

"Dear Nancy," the note reads in a rather shaky scrawl, "Thanks for the lovely lunch. Sorry I have to leave early. Love, Mary."

The mother contemplates the dirty dishes, the wrecked flower arrangement, the ruined day, grits her teeth again at the loud wailing of the kid upstairs, and flops herself down on the couch to cry her eyes out.

Bad scene. It's probably happened to most mothers.

When we know that our child may feel threatened by our attention to somebody else, we don't have to set it up for him to feel neglected, making it almost certain that his behavior will be impossible. We can let it be a day of special attention to him from the beginning.

Hire his favorite baby sitter to take him to the park for a picnic outing. Let him spend the night with a favorite aunt. Let him "help" with setting the table or sweeping the carport to get ready for the company. Go out of your way to give him a fair share of positive attention so he won't have to insist on the negative variety.

If he feels secure in our love, he can be his usual sweet self. But if he feels pushed aside and threatened, he'll naturally fight for his life in any way he knows how. None of the ways will be acceptable to us.

In setting behavior standards, as in the other areas of parenthood, we need to make frequent examinations of our motives.

One night at a church supper, I heard someone ask Debbie, "Do you like such-and-such a dish?"

Debbie made a perfectly awful face, looked as if she was going to heave-ho all her insides, and groaned, "Yuck, I hate it."

I was tempted to take her aside and tell her that next time anyone asked her a question like that she should politely say yes. But my motive would have been wrong.

We can see a little kid running up and down the hall of the church, and we can smile indulgently and think something sweet about how much energy the little dears have and how cute the kid is and all that. But when it's our kid, we grab ahold and swat him hard and give him a tongue lashing he won't soon forget.

"You know better than that! How many times have I told you never to run when you're inside a building—" and then we give him another swat.

We don't care if a neighbor's kid has dirty ears. We just give him a cookie and let him play until time to go home. But if we see a speck of wax in our kid's ears, we bless him out all over the place for being so filthy.

Far too often, pride and self are behind these unrealistic expectations of our own children. An honest self-examination might show us that we are requiring our children to function in certain behavioral patterns so people will praise us, saying, "Isn't she a wonderful parent? Her youngsters never talk back to her, never interrupt, never get mad, always obey. Her youngsters always says 'Yes, ma'am,' and 'No, sir,' and are *so* polite."

I worry about kids who are always superperfect, like puppets on a string who sweetly perform when we say, "Dance for our guests, honey." Someday, inevitably, the external pressure that has resulted in such perfection will be matched by an internal pressure that has to blow sky high to be released.

A young boy who had always had to toe an unreasonable mark of perfection at home went hog wild when he escaped to college. He did everything he could find a rule against, and was expelled from three institutions of higher learning in short order. His sister, subjected to the same kind of unreal external pressure at home, became a mental case within a few months of leaving home for good. She suffered through amnesia, not even recognizing her own mother when she came to see her. The outer manifestation of rejection reflected something that had been simmering inside her for years.

It's good for us to check our motives periodically and see whether some of our child's "misbehavior" is the result of our unrealistic, perfectionistic expectations.

12

Some Principles of Punishment

One summer afternoon I looked out the window and saw Danny's dog on the neighbors' lawn. They had pretty shrubbery, always kept their lawn neatly trimmed, and I knew they wouldn't want our dog playing on their grass.

"Danny," I called, "your dog is in the neighbor's yard. Go bring him home."

I heard Danny whistling and calling the dog, but after a little while he came in the kitchen where I was working, a woebegone look on his face.

"Did you get the dog?" I asked him.

"No, mom," he said, kind of hanging his head.

"Well, why not?" I wanted to know. "If he wouldn't come when you called him, why didn't you walk over and pick him up and carry him home?"

"Well, mom," he explained, "I'm not allowed to go in their yard."

"Not allowed to go in their yard? Why not? Their kids are always tromping through ours." An unrighteous indignation was welling up in me.

"Well—" He kind of shrugged his shoulders as if he didn't know the reason either. "I've just been forbidden to go on their lawn, that's all."

I tromped across the lawn to ring the neighbors' doorbell. *The very idea* that my boy couldn't set foot on their precious lawn—

Come to find out, Danny had thrown rocks at their little girl. Pretty good justification for telling him to keep out of their yard, I thought. I could understand, of course, why Danny hadn't bothered to tell me about that. I marched back home and dealt with him about the situation.

In a case like that, punishment was plainly called for, and I administered what I thought was proper. But we should never give our children the idea that they can't get by with *anything*. That's a devastating feeling. I have to be able to get by with a few things in order to live. My kids do, too.

If I was constantly in cahoots with the parents of every youngster on the block and my kids knew that absolutely everything they did was going to get ratted back to me, they'd find new friends in another part of town.

We need to let some things go by if they're not important and we can afford to overlook them. We can just breathe in and breathe out, be glad we know, but don't advertise everything. We don't have to deal with every minor infraction that we happen to learn about.

Taking a firm and consistent stand to punish what is really misbehavior that cannot be tolerated—throwing rocks at little girls—and overlooking the kind of rule violation that doesn't actually matter are two guidelines for happy and successful parenting.

This isn't just for the welfare of the child, it has real survival value for parents, too. If we can't turn our eyes away from some things that are admittedly less than perfect, our life will be used up in overmanaging our kids.

Another reason children need to get by with some things is so they won't have the feeling I had as a youngster—that an all-seeing eye was watching my every move. Today, many stores are peppered with little signs that say, "Warning to shoplifters: This store is equipped with closed-circuit TV." The signs may contain further weighty paragraphs detailing the awful things that happen to apprehended shoplifters.

Well, we have no intention of shoplifting anything when we go into the store, but with the signs watching our every move, we feel uncomfortably suspect the whole time we're there. We're almost afraid to open our purse to take out our shopping list for fear someone will think we're hiding stolen merchandise inside. It's as if the sign takes away our freedom to do right for the sake of doing right. In the same way, children too closely supervised have a hard time developing any integrity of their own.

There are many problem areas between parents and children that *ought* to be overlooked occasionally. Suppose our child doesn't want to eat all of the meat on his plate and so he sneaks a hunk of it to the dog under the table. That's probably not the time for an angry tirade about how hard we have to work to earn the money to put meat on the table. Neither is it the time to make the smallness of his appetite take the blame for the starving millions in India who would be glad for the tiniest morsel of food. It's probably the time for us to look out the window and pretend we don't notice

what's going on. We can be thankful that the kid loves the
dog instead of being angry that he doesn't like meatloaf
with onions in it. Failure to eat all the food on his plate is not
a life or death matter for the child. In fact, if he can learn *not*
to be a clean-plater, he may avoid obesity in later life.

I do not believe in forcing children to eat. Youngsters will
eat properly and sufficiently for their needs if the right
things are offered to them at appropriate times. Making a
child eat when he is not hungry creates many a mealtime
scene that should never have to take place. Some kids don't
need as much sleep as others; some don't need as much
food as others. We can't legislate appetite.

We can, however, do something about making sure that
our kids don't fall into the habit of exclusively eating snack-
type things that are just not nutritious enough. Such things
can take away their appetites for the nourishing foods their
bodies need to stay healthy, and there is even medical evidence that certain digestive disorders can result from a diet
that concentrates on very refined foods.

As the kids grow older, and are around the house less, we
can't keep a constant eye on their eating habits. But we can
make sure that home eating habits revolve around balanced
meals and healthful snacks like fresh fruits, nuts and the
like. Snack foods and candies can have their place as a part
of family celebrations like birthdays or as an occasional
accompaniment to TV watching—best of all, after a healthful, nutritious meal. It won't work to put snack foods on the
verboten list; that will just make them all the more attractive
once the kids get free of the rule. It's best to find a balance
and stick to it.

Mealtime should be a happy time. If kids spill their soup,
we can laugh about it with them. If they want only one meal
a day, that's all they need. It might hurt our feelings, our

pride, or our conscience to see them traipsing off to school in the morning munching on a handful of chocolate chip cookies, but if that's all they want, relax. If the child is satisfied, he's probably getting what he needs. If we're in doubt, we can let him have a daily vitamin pill.

Kids go through stages where they seem to eat nothing at all and then, all of a sudden, for no reason we can figure out, they're famished all the time.

If all punishment for not eating was repealed, think of the hassles in family life that would be avoided!

Just as there are some things called "misbehavior" that ought to be overlooked, there are other things that must never be overlooked but always dealt with.

"But how can you punish a kid today?" a man asked me recently, shrugging his shoulders in defeat. "My teenager is bigger than I am."

"Sir," I answered, "I don't buy that, and neither does God. But your teenager does because you've sold him on it. What you need to do is to start over, remembering that before God, you're still in control."

My mother, who was only five-feet-two-and-a-half, used to stand and look up at my six-foot-three brothers and say, "If I have to stand on one chair and use the other one on you, you're going to do what I say." She had a bluff and a half, and it worked. They believed her.

Have you ever said, "I wish my teenager wouldn't do thus or such a thing, but what can you do?" Have you been tempted to throw up your hands and quit?

I could always think of eight thousand things a discouraged parent might try. For a specific complaint, we can try a specific remedy, and if that one doesn't work, we can try another. If that doesn't work, we can come up with something else. As parents, we've got to become comfortable

with the realization that we are indeed placed in charge of
the lives of our children as long as they are dependent upon
us for their physical needs.

Sometimes kids come to me and complain, "My parents
are still trying to run my life, and I'm eighteen years old."

"Stop a minute," I tell them at the very beginning. "Do
you pay room and board?"

"Well, no," they answer more times than not.

"Are you working? Could you support yourself, pay your
own way?"

"Gosh, no. I'm still going to college."

"Then you'd better do what your parents tell you to do.
As long as you're dependent on them for your support,
you're subject to them in lots of other ways. When you want
to move out on your own, fine. In the meantime, follow
their rules in their house."

They usually get the point.

A mother came to me one day in complete despair about
her son. She said he acted as if he had a devil in him. There
was no father in the home, and the boy had thrown things at
his mother, broken the car windows, and done other de-
structive things deliberately.

"I just can't handle him," she cried.

When I offered to counsel with him, she told me that he
had refused to come for counseling, insisting there was
nothing wrong with him.

"Well," I said, "then about all you can do is pick up your
telephone and call the juvenile authorities."

She backed away from me in horror.

"Why, if I did that, he'd never speak to me again!" she
said.

"Well, then, go home and let him keep beating you up," I
told her, and she did.

That tyrant of a kid was ten years old! "I'm out of control!" was the frightening thing he saw about his own life. We can't afford to let that happen to our children.

Where both mother and father are working together for the common purpose of bringing their children up to maturity, they can punish misbehavior in ways exactly opposite and not harm their children by it.

For example, there can be a father who never punishes except with a spanking. Perhaps mother never spanks, but always uses verbal correction, a withdrawal of privileges, or maybe just raises an eyebrow or looks pained. Still, if the mother and father show respect for one another, upholding one another in whatever they do, and if they're bound together in love with the welfare of their youngsters at heart, it will be all right. The youngsters can understand that dad gives the lickings, that mom hands out the looks of displeasure, but the whole picture is one that gives the youngsters confidence and security in facing the world. They know somehow that they're being brought up right.

A father may say, "I'm not around enough. I let my wife handle the kids."

Or a mother may say, "I'm not strong enough. I let dad do it all."

It doesn't matter who dishes out the punishment, just as long as it gets dished out.

Sometimes a father will come in and make a big declaration, really laying down the law, and then take off leaving mother to see that an overly-harsh edict is carried out. That's less than ideal. Whenever possible, the parent imposing the punishment should be the one to see that it's enforced.

Are you a parent who finds it difficult to inflict physical punishment on your youngster? If it's hard for you, maybe you have a tendency to go overboard. Maybe you're the kind of mom or dad who has to leave a welt, who has to use a board, who thinks that if you really beat a child good one time, all your problems with him will be over and you'll never have to punish him for anything again.

If that's how you're thinking, think again.

There isn't anything that alleviates guilt more quickly than a good old-fashioned spanking. But a brutal beating is never necessary. The amount of pain inflicted is not the measure of whether or not we've gotten our message across. If we've brought tears, if we've broken the rebellion, we've won, whether it took one spank or fifteen.

In spanking, our goal should be to establish a conditioned reflex in the child that says, "What I did was wrong. If I do it again, this will happen again. I don't want this consequence, so I won't engage in that action."

We don't have to spank our youngsters while we're still infuriated at what they've done. We can give ourselves a little time to cool down first.

After our emotions are under control, we are ready to spank in order to correct the child, not to dispel our anger. Then we won't feel guilty for correcting the child.

Sometimes the youngster we've just spanked comes up to us and wants a hug immediately afterward. Will our loving him up verbally and by a physical expression of affection make him think his wrong behavior was right after all? No. Actually, refusal to hug a child after we have administered a spanking will give him the erroneous impression that we love him only when he is pleasing us. He needs to know that our love is a constant thing, a love that keeps on loving no matter what he's done.

Post-spanking time is an ideal time for positive rein-forcement, for cementing love, drawing the child close and explaining that the punishment was meted out because we love him and want him to do right so he'll grow up to be a happy person.

After they get a little older, children are less immediately forgiving of us for punishing them. They might find it difficult to receive our love, much less express any of their own. But an expression of love from us won't minimize the effectiveness of the correction. It will actually help the child of whatever age to be more obedient, because he'll want to please us. We can make it clear that we've punished him because we don't want him consigned to a life of frustration and unfulfillment.

Punishment for rebellion, for breaking known rules, should always have a direct relation to the offense. If, for example, our youngster is supposed to be in at ten o'clock and his teenage group persuades him to stay out until eleven, it would be well for us to let him make up the time by putting a nine o'clock limit on the next outing. If that works, fine. If not, sterner measures are in order—maybe a denial of the going-out privilege the next time he wants to go somewhere. A consistent reward for keeping a rule, and a consistent withdrawal of privilege for violating it, will achieve the result for which we are aiming.

We can use a lesser punishment for a first offense than for subsequent instances of the same kind of misbehavior. For example, if our child has never stolen anything before, and one day a playmate talks him into taking a half dollar out of our purse to buy ice cream cones, we don't have to take drastic measures. For a first offense, we can explain why taking the money without consulting us was wrong, tell the child he is never to take money from our purse again without permission, and let him go. If the same "crime" occurs again, it's time for some form of correction.

The punishment should be fair. It should not be unduly restrictive or severe. It should be only as harsh as it needs to be to correct the behavior pattern.

We'll never go in for the "you're grounded for a month" kind of punishment if we put ourselves in our child's shoes. He will have to live with the restriction for thirty days. That can seem like eternity and give him a hopeless, what's-the-use attitude.

If our youngster has misused the car privilege, we can take the car keys away, but if he has misused the telephone privilege, we don't take the car keys away. Imposing the same punishment for a variety of different offenses lets the child grow up thinking that every breach of conduct is a mortal sin, that every time he's wrong, it's a national emergency. It's important to keep punishment within a sensible perspective. An accidental mishap should not carry the same penalty as an act of deliberate, malicious destruction.

What if our child throws a tantrum to get his way? In the first place, we should never reward him by giving him what he wanted. If we reward tantrum behavior, he'll have tantrums with increasing frequency.

In the second place, we shouldn't hang around to watch the tantrum. We should walk away from it. Deprived of an audience, tantrums go away more quickly than with any other action.

We'd be well-advised to pray when an irate father decides to take a too-firm hand in punishing a child. If he goes at it with a grim approach, "One good licking will straighten out all his behavior problems for all time," we can get out of sight and on our knees. That kind of adult tantrum is best handled by depriving it of an audience, too.

To me, lying is one of the worst forms of misbehavior. If I can count on what my youngsters tell me to be the truth, I go easier on their punishment. I encourage my youngsters to admit their wrongdoing. That doesn't mean that I fail to punish them, but I always reward the honesty somehow.

"Danny, I want you to know that I really appreciate your telling me the truth about what happened. You know that you were in the wrong, but now help me decide what we should do about it to keep this kind of thing from happening again."

In every case that has come to my attention, the child has suggested a far harsher punishment than the parent would have thought of imposing.

Kids are hard on themselves. They're likely to say, "Well, all my privileges should be taken away for a week, and I should have to do all the chores around the house, and I shouldn't get an allowance for a whole month—"

What such suggestions say to us is, "Mom, I have a tremendous load of guilt about what I did wrong, and harsh discipline will relieve me of some of it."

What are we supposed to do with our feelings when our youngster has gone absolutely contrary to all that we've required of him, when he has ridden roughshod over all our careful training? It's natural to get mad.

Some parents have gotten the impression that they should never get mad, never show resentment, never exhibit hostility toward their youngster no matter what he does. That's unreal. More times than not, such parents end up leaving the child free to suit himself. He can break their standards, tear down their home, beat on his younger brothers and sisters, and they never respond with a normal, instinctive reaction of anger.

Is that an ideal we should strive toward? Never.

When I'm mad, my kids know I'm mad. They know why I'm mad, too, because I tell them.

Sometimes I say to them, "Don't talk to me right now, because I'm mad."

They get out of my way, believe me. Now, they don't feel rejected when I tell them that. They recognize that I'm reacting to a situation, not to them.

Some parents attempt to handle their anger by simply not speaking to the child. They pout in their corner, without any explanation, and the child naturally picks up a rejection message. It's better, when we're mad, to say so. The child can cope with that. He can't cope with what happens inside him when he thinks, "Mom doesn't love me any more."

Little youngsters bite sometimes, and instead of teaching them not to bite, some parents bite back, and slap back. Terrible as that is, an emotional war is even worse.

"Well, you didn't say goodbye to mommy, so mommy isn't going to say goodbye to you." Or, "You don't think I'm so wonderful, so I don't think you're so wonderful." This kind of rejection is the most damaging thing that can happen to a youngster. It makes him reject himself.

In dealing with children, we're dealing with indescribably tender emotional babies. We can't afford to play tit for tat with them, because everything that goes to make up their emotions and their egos is lying wide open, just as if we had split them down the middle and turned them wrong side out. They're completely exposed, totally vulnerable. It doesn't take more than a dirty look from us to crush them. At the same time, they may act as if they couldn't care less. They may even say, "Yech. Here we go again," but on the inside, they're saying something else, something that sounds like, "Mamma, I hurt."

When one of our youngsters has caused anger in us, we

shouldn't try to satisfy our feelings with a couple of little numbers on the piano, pretending that nothing is wrong. There's a cloud hanging over our relationship. We can't ignore it. We have to deal with it.

If, when the storm is calmed, we've decided not to punish this time, we ought to tell the child the score so he'll know where he stands and not be afraid we're going to lower the boom any second.

"Honey, what you did was wrong. I never want it to happen again. But it's over and done with, and I'm not holding it against you."

Our child is suddenly set free to heave a sigh of relief along with us and to do better next time without a threat hanging over his head. Then we can pray with him:

"Lord, we just come to You and thank You that You died for us on the cross, that You have borne all our sins. Thank You, Lord, that no matter what sins we've committed, You still love us, and when we come to You, You wash all our sins away. You make us clean, and You don't hold anything against us. Thank You that we won't even remember our sins any more. They'll all be gone."

When we have closed the prayer, we can say to our youngster, "It's so good to be free, isn't it? Now, let's both walk in freedom." After punishment or a decision not to punish, it's a time for starting over with a clean slate.

Sometimes parents try to pay the price for their youngsters, to take all the frustration, all the pain, all the responsibility for their kids' actions upon themselves. But it doesn't work. It can't be done.

Children brought up in such an atmosphere have a hard time maturing because they have the attitude, "All parents are wrong. All adults owe me a living. Other people are responsible for my misdeeds—it's all their fault."

We help our youngsters learn from their mistakes when we punish them for misbehavior. That's what punishment is all about. Once we understand that, we'll stick with it until we have accomplished our purpose as parents who love our children and want the best in life for them.

13

Discipline, Freedom, and Responsibility

Some of the biggest problems in family relationships occur in the area of discipline. In its broadest sense, discipline is preventive. If we handle preventive discipline properly, there will be less need for the kind that is more often termed punishment. *Webster's Collegiate Dictionary* defines "discipline" as "training that corrects, molds, or perfects the mental faculties or moral character; punishment; control gained by forcing obedience or order."

Our paramount goal in disciplining our youngsters is to mold in them the character or behavior that will be of greatest benefit to them during the growing-up years and on through adulthood. Our motive in disciplining our children properly is that they might come to mature, responsible, and enjoyable adulthood of their own, fulfilling to the fullest the potential God has placed within them. If we do our job properly, our children will emerge as effectively self-disciplined adults.

Good discipline begins when a child is very young. By our actions, we train our children to be obedient the first time we tell them to do something—or we train them to stall until we yell at them the umpteenth time with a loud voice, fierce threats, and rising blood pressure. We make our choice here, wittingly or unwittingly, by whether or not we follow through with enforcing our requirements as soon as they are given.

Good discipline is a relief to a youngster, relief from the responsibility of managing his own life before he's old enough to do it with wisdom. Deciding what is right and what is wrong is an unbearable burden in the life of a child. This burden falls inevitably on children who have to grow up without a home, but tragically, the same weight is often felt in allegedly Christian homes where the children are provided for in material ways but otherwise live as if they have no parents.

It's always easier to do a thing ourselves than to teach our children to do it properly. But that's not the point. The point is that we need to discipline our youngsters, not require them to discipline us.

At the table one night, I was eating my second helping of dessert, and Debbie caught me at it.

"Neat diet, mom," she said, wagging a finger at me. "Two pieces of pie—"

Naturally I tried to defend myself. "I dieted at breakfast," I told her.

"Now listen," she scolded. "I don't want you going without breakfast. Breakfast is—"

"—the most important meal of the day." I finished it with her.

We both laughed, but as I thought it over later, I realized how easy it is for a youngster to fall into the role of being responsible for her parents, and it's awfully easy for us parents to let it happen. But it's not fair to the children. And it's not God's best for us, either.

It's sad to see adults who were never allowed to be children because they were always having to wait on someone or be responsible for them. The resulting frustration comes out in a lot of ways—rebellion, misbehavior, running away, marrying too early, becoming promiscuous, never marrying. Somewhere in their life, children who were made to grow up too fast are going to have to fight feelings of resentment toward the parents who let it happen, who forced them into an adult role too soon.

There are, of course, parents who go to the opposite extreme, parents who never let their kids grow up, who keep them always infants. This is unnatural. Kids want to grow up. From the time a baby is two years old, he doesn't want to be a baby any more. He wants to be a big boy; she wants to be a big girl.

Early in their lives, we have to begin to allow our offspring to express some independence lest we begin to suppress it so effectively that they begin to take on a perpetual baby role. Perpetual babies grow up physically but remain so emotionally insecure that they're afraid to tackle anything for fear they'll do it wrong. They're likely to be people who think the world owes them a living because their parents always gave them what they needed without disciplining them to effect growth in responsibility.

With the speed of the lives we live today, there's not a whole lot of disciplining being done in some families. Everyone is rushing around all the time. If the only way we can spend time in our home with our youngster is to drop something else we're doing, we'd better drop it, no matter how worthy the cause. There's got to be some regular disciplining done in our home or our kids will suffer.

Do our youngsters know that they're *supposed* to be responsible for cleaning their room, but their attitude is, "Aw, don't worry. Mom will do it"? Do they know that they should hang up their clothes when they take them off in order to cut down on the washing and ironing we have to do? Or do they throw everything on the floor or in the laundry basket because they know we'll take care of it for them?

Being a good parent doesn't mean being a doormat for our children. Being a doormat for them doesn't equip them for living in the world out there. They have to be disciplined to do things for themselves, because the world isn't going to wait on them.

We have to let our youngsters know what we expect from them. If we expect them to help around the house, they should know it. If we expect them to mind, they should know it. If we expect too much, we won't get it. The goals we set must be realistic and reachable, so approval can come, so our children can grow in love and maturity.

Sometimes we fall into the trap of thinking that our children are automatically going to grow up knowing everything that we know, everything we had to learn the hard way. But it doesn't happen like that. They have to be taught. They have to be disciplined.

Much of our disciplining of our youngsters is in connection with the basic needs in their lives. In some homes, it doesn't matter how hungry a youngster gets, he isn't permitted to eat anything until mealtime. In others, the kid can eat all day long.

Which is right?

Either way will do, as long as we are consistent instead of confusing.

When our youngster comes in and whines, "But, mom, I'm starved to death," we might let him eat right then or we might tell him, "I'm sorry, but supper won't be ready for an hour yet."

In the first case, we're teaching him that he can have what he wants when he wants it. In the second case, we're teaching him control, not indulgence, helping him learn that he can't succumb to the desire to eat, just because he is hungry.

Most normal children fuss about doing their chores at one time or another. But chores should be done, not merely to have the work accomplished but for what the discipline of regular chores does toward bringing a child to responsible maturity.

My son has to keep his room clean. But he keeps it clean according to his standards, not mine. He's required to make his bed every day, and to pick up anything lying on the floor. I know that his drawers are filled with papers that ought to be thrown out, and that his puzzles are never put back together, but if they're out of sight, I don't complain. He knows where to find what he needs. To me, the room is not clean. To him, it is. Every once in a while, I go in with him and we have a real throwing-out day. Tons of junk gets gone. But in the meantime, we have a workable compromise.

Responsibilities for chores around the house need to decrease as the child's responsibilities outside the home increase. But the letting down needs to come from us. We can explain to the whole family, "Now that Tommy is working, he has to get up early, and he's so tired when he gets home that we're not going to expect him to mow the lawn this summer."

We let the job pass to a younger member of the family whose schedule isn't so crowded.

When the younger children gripe about this—and they will—we remind them that their turn is coming, when they'll be freed from some household chore for the same reason. That makes it a little easier for them to take, and helps them look forward to the time when they can go out to get a job instead of having to hang around the house to baby-sit and wash dishes. In the meantime, underneath the complaining, they're secretly proud of being promoted to a new level of responsibility themselves.

Freedom is an essential part of the teaching of responsibility and self-discipline. There must always be flexibility in freedom to adapt to new situations, to new stages of the growth in maturity of your child. Often, I have found myself giving my youngsters more freedom in a certain area than they were capable of managing responsibly. For example, I'd say, "Danny, I want this, that, and the other thing done sometime tomorrow."

He'd give me a sweet, "Okay, mom," but if I didn't mention the things again the next morning, when evening came I'd find they hadn't been taken care of. Then I'd realize that the freedom I'd given him was still beyond the level of his self-discipline. I'd have to step in and start over, saying, "Danny, I want you to do thus and such a thing *right now*." He did it, and we both learned something.

We shouldn't be afraid to broaden our child's freedom and then to narrow it back down again when we see that we've erred. Next time, our child might surprise us by showing that he can be trusted with a greater latitude of responsibility. It's a matter of constant adjustment, continual testing. We have to make our standards more exacting when we see the youngster getting slack with his own.

If we're riding horseback, and the horse turns away from

the road, we pull the reins in for a while, but we don't keep him tightly reined for the rest of his life. To bring him to maturity, we trust him a little again, release our hold a little. If he starts to run away another time, we rein him in once more. The whole object is to get him self-disciplined so that he'll walk at just the right pace and in just the right direction to take us safely home even if we fall asleep and let the reins fall from our hands.

Some parents ride too free or too tight all the time, never releasing or tightening their hold on their youngsters to suit the circumstances. The child concludes either, "I can't do anything," or, "My folks don't care *what* I do." There is a happy medium of sensible government with our children.

If we have a little one, and we begin to trust him with something, we need to remember to praise him for his achievement. We don't saddle him with too much responsibility all at once, but let him work up to it gradually so he can succeed, building up our confidence in him and his own confidence in himself. If he fails, we don't condemn him, but see if we can find and remedy the cause of his failure. There may be a legitimate reason for it that is not his fault at all.

What if we tell our child to do something, and he nicely agrees to do it and heads in that general direction but never quite arrives at the destination? Parents usually get quite frustrated about such things. We may not want to be legalistic about it, but when a child is supposed to clean his room every Saturday and he neglects it three weeks in a row, we begin to think of dire measures.

A good rule to follow here, to keep from getting into situations that make our blood boil, is first, to make firm rules only about those things that are really important to us.

Second, let teens plan their own schedules as much as possible.

For instance, instead of saying, "I want you to clean your room on Saturday afternoon between two and four o'clock," we can say, "I want your room cleaned before you go anywhere or do anything else next weekend." Then the youngster can make his own schedule and reap the benefits of having his chores done on time—or the penalties of not completing them according to schedule.

The object, again, is not so much to get the jobs accomplished as to use them to help the child achieve the self-discipline of responsible adulthood.

There should be a consequence if our time limit is not met. Children need to know that it is always necessary for someone to "pay the piper." We will help them by being relatively inflexible about this. We're training them so that they won't be fired from their first job for procrastination. Young people have to learn somewhere to "get on with it," and home is the best place.

During the early teens, children need to be reminded consistently before they reap the consequences of their failure to accomplish something. They may call it nagging, but we should do it anyway so that they won't come up to the deadline facing a penalty they forgot they would encounter. After fifteen or so, it's time to stop reminding and let them take the consequences of their failure to complete an assignment. Somewhere they have to learn to be responsible for their own follow-through—without our reminder. That helps them learn that there is a direct relationship between fulfilling responsibilities and enjoying privileges.

I'm a great believer in letting teenagers have as much freedom as possible. They cannot be held in close restraint without rebelling against it, inwardly or outwardly.

If we are determined to hold the reins tightly, to be all powerful, always to have the last word, to be considered infallible just because we are mother or father, we will never enjoy a right relationship with our teenagers.

On the other hand, our kids will move smoothly into self-disciplined adulthood if we have helped them learn by experience that a proper fulfilling of responsibilities is a necessary prerequisite to freedom.

Some of the problems parents have in disciplining their children arise because the youngsters do not see the blessedness of discipline while it is going on. When we ourselves are being disciplined, we don't see the blessedness of it either. And yet we discipline our children and expect them to bounce right back with a big hug and an "I love you, mommy. Thank you for making me clean my room. Thank you for not letting me go to the movie until after I've mowed the lawn."

When, instead of such a loving response from our kids, we see a little pouting, or hear their bedroom door slam, or see or hear any other outward form of rebellion, we may store it up in our minds and find ourselves reluctant to discipline the next time it's needed.

We have to guard against our reaction to their reaction. That a child rebels against discipline doesn't mean that he doesn't need it. He probably needs more of it—to instill in him habits of self-discipline.

Some of us go to the other extreme, staying on the defensive, declaring, "I don't care whether you like this or not, this is the way it's going to be." Such a dogmatic attitude can close the doors of communication. The situation may get steadily worse until a major eruption occurs and the child runs away from home or does something else to demonstrate his rejection of his family.

There are parents who ignore a lot of undesirable behavior in their youngsters because they simply don't know
what to do about it. Recently I talked with a father and after
I had expressed my honest love and concern for his child,
the father asked if I would follow through with enforcing
the necessary discipline on his offspring. This is an extreme
example of a parent expecting the school or some other
agency to bring up his kids for him, discipline and all.

We have to overcome the maternal instinct that says, "I
want to do everything for this child." We have to get to the
point where we can say, "Lord, I know this is not my child.
She belongs to you. Help her to get from me everything she
needs to become a healthy, happy, well-adjusted,
independent individual. And then enable me to let her live
her own life."

Far more difficult than the proper nurturing of a child is
the timely weaning of him. We all know how that goes. We
set the date, maybe even mark it on the calendar: "This is
the day when the bottle goes!"

But junior has other ideas. He says, "That's what *she*
thinks. I love my bottle, and I'm going to hold onto it for a
while yet."

And he gets his way. At two o'clock in the morning, after
fighting it out all day long, we give up, fill the bottle, and
crawl back to bed, full of the exhaustion of defeat. Maybe
our motive—to have him weaned because the neighbor's
kid was weaned already—didn't fit his need. When that is
true, our efforts at discipline are sure to fail.

We never outgrow the need for self-discipline. If we
didn't discipline ourselves, we wouldn't hold a job, we
wouldn't clean house, rake the leaves, get up early, read the

Bible, or do a lot of other things that are vital to our well-being.

If we can help our youngsters to see that discipline is a necessary part of life and that achieving self-discipline is more satisfactory than being disciplined by others, we'll have given them a strong motivation for maturity. If they see us disciplining ourselves, they'll have fewer resentments in areas where they have to be disciplined.

When a youngster says, "I don't want to go to school today. I'm sick of school," we can say, "I know just how you feel. I don't want to go to work either. But we've both got to do it. Have another glass of milk and let's go." It's good for kids to see that we are self-disciplined and that they can be, too.

One reason why we have more trouble with disciplining a child than with disciplining ourselves is that we're so accustomed to disciplining ourselves, we do it automatically. On the other hand, when we have to discipline our youngsters, we are always aware—sometimes painfully so—of what we're doing. We need to be reminded that the Scripture says, "Whom he loveth, he chasteneth," and what is true between God and man is true also between earthly parents and their offspring.

Oftentimes parents, because we're so close to our teenagers, get discouraged, not realizing that real growth is taking place in them. If we could back up and get a little perspective, we'd see better what is happening.

If we want our kids to grow up, we have to discipline ourselves to progressively take our hands off them. We have to let them make some mistakes, do some wrong things, on their own. They learn by doing. And so do we.

14

Encouraging Maturity

We need to instill in our youngsters a personal integrity platform of their own, because the day will come when we won't be with them to decide yes or no. They will have to make decisions for themselves when mom and dad aren't around for a consultation.

If a junior high school youngster asks, "Mom, why can't I do such-and-such," and the answer is simply, "Because I said not," we haven't helped him grow to maturity. We have provoked him to frustration instead.

A teenager came to me and said, "It doesn't make any difference why I want to do something, no matter how I lay it out to my parents, they always say no. When I ask why, they answer, 'Just because we said so.' " The youngster was understandably confused and at sea about how to make decisions for himself when his parents weren't around to help him.

In the old-fashioned family home, when parents said, "I said so because I said so," they could get by with it. But not today. Kids want reasons.

The days of "Because I said so" are over. We are in an intellectual era, not an authoritarian one. No teacher is teaching on the basis of "Because I said so." Teachers are proving everything to our youngsters and expecting the youngsters to prove things back to them. Pupils aren't expected to take the teacher's word for anything. Explanation is the order of the day.

In math, they are proving that with a base of one, one and one equals two. In physics and chemistry, they're giving reasons for their formulas. Everything is being approached from the standpoint of reason, not simple memorization.

Parents need to be aware of this significant change in teaching methods. When children go to school all day learning the whys and being expected to prove them, they're programmed to want explanations from parents, too, instead of accepting the old "Because I said so" routine. If we don't give them a why, they'll keep trying to find one. And if they can't find a why that satisfies them, they'll be tempted to be disobedient.

In addition to explaining *our* whys to our youngsters, it's good if we ask them the whys of *their* actions. We shouldn't ask why when we really mean, "I don't like what you did." We shouldn't, for instance, say, "Why did you come in with mud on your shoes?" We should tell them instead, "Clean the mud off your shoes." But we should ask why when we want to know why.

We can discuss the why of misbehavior with children old enough to think things through. We can ask them their motives, and try to follow their line of reasoning.

"I did it because I wanted to" is a real answer, but not a very helpful one. Don't stop there.

"Son, let's look at what doing what you wanted cost you."

As we pursue that dialogue, we're training our youngster to look at the consequences of his wrong actions. He will see what it cost this person and that one, his parents, and himself. Then we can ask, "Now, son, what would you have done differently if you'd thought of all these things ahead of time?"

If we lead our child through this kind of look at his own behavior, we'll have helped him toward more mature action and responsibility in the future.

A twenty-three-year-old boy was asking me one day about some of the laws in the Old Testament.

"I don't understand why a God of love would lay down some of those laws," he said. "They sound so ridiculous to me. Don't eat this, don't eat that—"

He thought most of the Old Testament laws were arbitrary and dictatorial until I showed him that every law God put in the Bible was a protection to His people. Even what seem to us silly little laws about how food is to be prepared were given to prevent sickness.*

When the boy realized this, he began to understand that there is a reason for everything God wants in our lives. The commandment that children are to honor their father and mother is a good example. This rule isn't in the Bible for the purpose of making parents feel honored. When children learn to honor and obey their parents, they learn to honor and obey others who have the rule over them, and their lives

---

* For a helpful explanation, see *None of These Diseases,* by Dr. S.I. McMillen (Spire Books, 1967).

are naturally smoother and happier.

Kids are helped toward maturity if they know the whys of our actions and our rules. I'm not saying that knowing our whys will make them agree with us, necessarily. But knowing our whys makes certain things easier for them to take.

I can say, "Danny, please bring in some kindling and a load of logs for the fireplace."

"Why do *I* have to do it?" he gripes. "Why can't Debbie do it?"

I have a good answer for that, and I give it to him.

"Debbie just did the dishes; you bring in the wood."

He does it. Maybe he doesn't *look* any happier about it, but at least he has a reason to satisfy his mind.

The necessity for expressing a reason makes us examine our own motives continually. That's helpful, too.

Our child needs to learn that he can't change our mind by teasing to get his own way about something. At such times, we'll help him most by letting our *no* be *no*—henceforth and forevermore. If he learns that if he begs and teases long enough, he can wear us down and get his own way, he's learned something very dangerous to his development into maturity.

Children who always get their own way through manipulation are being rewarded for manipulating, and they'll use it increasingly against their parents and everywhere else it will work.

But there are problems, too, where a parent is so unbending that he never changes his mind.

Good parents are not afraid to change their minds. After we've listened and heard the child's point of view about something, we ought to be able to admit, if it's true, that we've made a mistake. We should explain why we've changed our minds or suspended a rule. The whole business of rules and discipline doesn't go down the drain just because we make an occasional exception.

When as parents we are interested only in our word being infallible law forever and ever without change, we need to look at our own security, our self-confidence, our sense of worth as individuals. Inflexibility is not a quality of good parenthood. Changing the rules for special circumstances lets our children see that we really care about them, not just about our rules. It may give them more respect for our judgment, too.

If we are habitually inconsistent and double-minded, of course, this will water down our authority in the mind of the child. But that is not to say the same thing will happen when, for instance, we've told a child he can't go to a certain place and then we get more information that makes us decide to let him go. We can explain why we've changed our mind, and the child won't be left hanging in mid-air, thinking we're wishy-washy.

Our changed mind should come from our thinking about a situation, getting more information, not from our youngster's begging to have his own way. Kids who get their own way by wheedling and begging are a menace to their parents, their families, their communities, and most tragic of all, to themselves. But a mind that is never changed is in the same category as socks or bedsheets that stay put forever. Who wants them?

As we mature in our Christian growth, one of the first things that happens to us is that we become more open, better able to admit our mistakes, better able to listen to the evidence and opinion of others without reacting defensively. And as this happens to us, in full view of our youngsters, it happens to them, too.

15

Your Kids and Their Attitudes

The subject of parental duties and responsibilities is a controversial one. It's easy for us to become frustrated by the conflicting opinions of the experts. One expert believes one thing, and he "proves" his theory. Another expert believes something exactly opposite, and he "proves" his theory, too.

The proper balance often lies between the two extremes. We need to judge all teaching for ourselves. Whenever any teaching becomes uncomfortable to us, we should examine it closely to see if God is putting His endorsement on it or if it's just an idea of men. Not all teachings that claim to come from God have Him as their source.

Many have turned their backs on the written Word of God as a guide in child-rearing. "This is a new era," they say.

"We are a new generation."

Times do change, but the Word of God is never out of date. It is only our application of it that is behind the times. The legalistic approach that many have used for so long is outmoded. The Lord is showing us today, as Jesus showed the scribes and Pharisees of His day, that He is interested in dealing with attitudes rather than with legalistic specifics.

Society says, "Hold your children very loose. Do not force on your youngster your own ideas, your ideals, the things that were forced on you as you grew up."

The Bible doesn't agree. In Proverbs 29:15 we read, "The rod and reproof give wisdom: but a child left to himself bringeth his mother to shame."

In view of the contrast between society and Scripture— the way the world does things as opposed to the way God tells us to do them—we need to examine the difference for ourselves and see which way results in the best possible life for our children.

There's no question that we are in this society. We can't depart from it mentally or physically unless we can shoot ourselves to the moon and stay there. We're here, like it or not, and the things that go on about us are going to influence our lives and the way we bring up our children.

When my children were small, I didn't remove all the knickknacks from the coffee table; I taught my kids no-no. They learned it. Because the world *is* with us, we still have to teach our children no-no.

It should be obvious that children cannot be trusted to raise themselves—they're too young, they lack experience and wisdom. And yet in many American homes today, apparently, the children are expected to assume total responsibility for how they turn out. Some modern parents have embraced society's attitude that they are responsible for seeing that their children are fed, clothed, sheltered, herded off to school Monday through Friday, to the recreation park on Saturday, to Sunday school on Sunday morning, and that parental responsibility ends there.

The results of that kind of parental irresponsibility fill the dockets of juvenile court sessions.

God's promise, in the other hand, is that if parents will train up a child in the way he should go, when he is old he will not depart from it. The Bible says it is a parent's responsibility to get into his youngsters what he believes is right, to teach the laws of God diligently to his children (Deut. 6:7).

Have you ever heard your youngster say, "So-and-so does such-and-such, but we don't, do we, mommy?" The child is acknowledging his faithfulness to the training you have given him. Mother's and dad's platform has become his own. He knows it's right for him to do this and wrong for him to do that.

There was one area of my own upbringing that was one-sided and legalistic. I was quite a grown-up girl before I found out that some nice people drink alcoholic beverages. Good people, moral people, people who are honest. Learning that was a real shock to my system because my parents' platform said, "All people who drink are bad, and no good people drink." They hadn't said it in so many words, but I believed it because of the way I had been brought up.

What we say to our children has a greater impact on them than what any teacher, any other child, or anyone else says. It's true that at certain ages they may seem to care more about the attitudes of their peers than about ours, but this doesn't last forever.

A twenty-five-year-old youth came in to see me one day. He had grown up in a Christian home that had taught the Word of God but had stressed legalistic don'ts—"Don't smoke, don't drink, don't swear, don't do this and don't do that." He had rebelled against it all one day, and had walked away from it.

"Now," he said, "I do all these things, but there's no joy in them for me. I'm going crazy in the midst of them. I can't really get it out of my mind that all these things are wrong." The boy had rebelled against his parents' teaching, but it was still there inside him, an integral part of him. He would never find happiness until he could weigh his previous training in the light of his current convictions centered in the Word of God. Only then would his inner warfare be gone.

It is God who has arranged for parental influence to be so strong that if we say a thing, it becomes fact in the minds of our children. They will never forget what mom and dad believed, even if someone "proves" it wrong.

There is a difference between verbal instruction called teaching and what we call training. Our English word "train" means "to bring to a requisite standard, as of a conduct or skill, by protracted and careful instruction; specifically, to mold the character of." The Hebrew word *chanak* comes from a primary root word which means "to narrow."

When we train our children up in the way they should go, we have carved our children, we have molded their character by narrowing them, by disciplining them. Such training involves far more than merely telling a child what's right and wrong.

It has been established that we retain ten percent of what we hear, fifty percent of what we hear and see, and eighty percent of what we hear, see, and participate in. This is why teachers use pictures, flannelgraphs, movies, and other kinds of visual aids in instruction.

If we really want to train our youngsters, to effectively mold their characters, we have to let them hear from our lips, see in our lives, and learn through their own participation all that we want them to know. If what they see in our lives is not consistent with what they hear from our lips, we're in trouble.

Suppose we want to train our child to love animals. We are training him when we say, "We don't hurt animals, we love them," and follow that up by treating our household pets with loving kindness. If, however, we permit the child to kick his dog, he will not suddenly learn to love animals. Our training must follow through in every stage.

We train our children to love—or not to love—their parents in the same way. When we say to our child, "Love daddy," and show love toward daddy ourselves, we are reinforcing our teaching. But if we say to our child, "You should love your daddy," and then behave in unloving ways toward him ourselves, we shouldn't be surprised if the child says, "Why should I love daddy? You don't."

Actions always speak louder than words in teaching right attitudes.

Social workers trying to understand what's happened in a home will often observe children when they are playing house. They learn surprising things this way, getting some real insights into the kind of home children come from.

The little kid who's always beating the other kid tells them something. And the one who's always promising the little doll that she'll be right back tells them something else.

One little six-year-old boy revealed a lot about the kind of love in the home he came from when he was playing by himself one day in his grandmother's house. He had taken a pile of clothes from the laundry basket and was pretending to iron them on the hearth. When his grandmother passed through the room, he looked up at her and explained, "I don't usually do the ironing, but my wife's pregnant." The grandmother chuckled, assured that there was loving helpfulness in the boy's home.

If we tell our children they should be good to those who persecute them and they see us always trying to get even with our enemies, they'll be confused about what is really required. "If you talk it, walk it," is a good rule to follow. What they hear us say and what they see us do has to fall in line.

When Debbie was very young, I began to show her pictures of uniformed policemen.

"If you ever get lost," I told her, "find a nice policeman to help you."

The words I spoke to her were just right, conveying exactly what I wanted to teach her and showing a proper respect for authority. But one day she made me realize that by my influence and example, I was teaching something else, loud and clear. She couldn't miss it—and she didn't.

Whenever I was out driving my car, maybe crowding the speed limit a little, I'd let up on the accelerator when I saw a policeman or a patrol car.

"Whoops! There's a flatfoot," I'd say, not meaning to undermine my deliberate teaching, but doing it just the same. One day when Debbie was about three years old, she was standing in the front seat beside me—we didn't have seat belts in those days—when she happened to spot a policeman on the corner before I did.

"Oh, oh mommy," she warned me. "Better slow down. There's a 'fatfoot.' "

I began right then to mend my ways. If I wanted my child to grow up as a law-abiding citizen, I'd have to be one myself. Debbie would have to see me adhering to the laws of the land whether there was any "fatfoot" on the corner or not.

Once when I had been away on a prolonged speaking trip, I came home to learn that Dan had acquired a couple of speeding tickets. I talked to him about them and about the necessity for obeying the law on the highway as well as everywhere else. It didn't matter that he thought the limit was too low, I said. He had to obey it anyway, because it was the law.

I didn't impose any disciplinary measures at that time, but a few days later, when he came in with a third ticket, I knew I had to take action.

"One more ticket, Danny," I told him, "and you'll have to give me the keys to your car."

I went with Danny to court, and when the judge learned what I had said about the speeding offenses, he let Danny off with a small fine. The privilege of having a car to drive had to lead to an attitude of increased responsibility for obeying the motor vehicle laws. Dan learned it.

Children also learn right attitudes of patriotism and national responsibility by the attitudes we express verbally and through our actions. It takes real discipline not to be constantly running down our nation these days. When I pick up the newspaper, I groan from the first page through the last one night after night. It's traumatic for me to read it. I have to go out of my way to try to instill in my youngsters a realization that for every negative there is in America, we should thank God for a whole lot of positives. I try to make my kids glad they're Americans, that they live in a country where they can choose their own employment and worship God as they choose. I let them know that most of the rest of the world can't take such blessings for granted the way we do.

To teach our children responsible citizenship and a love for their country, we have to live it ourselves.

In wartime, we ought to say to our sons, "Be the best soldier you can be for Jesus Christ and for your country."

If Debbie ever has to wait at home while her husband goes off to war, I want to say to her, "Be brave about it—because he's going to fight for the best country on the face of the earth."

In war or in peace, our children need to have a strong national pride, for their sake and for the sake of our nation. The most important, lasting, single influence on their attitude in every area of life is what they see in us.

The role of family traditions in teaching and training attitudes is another powerful one.

Grandmas seem to love tradition, to enjoy doing their thing with their grandchildren to keep family traditions intact to be passed on to a next generation. Often mothers are too preoccupied with other things to go to the bother of making Christmas cookies with the little people. There are times when we don't seem to realize that the mess of flour all over the kitchen floor can be swept up, and that opportunities to make lasting, loving memories in the lives of our children are limited to a few brief years.

My mom always let us kids help make Christmas cookies . . . hang Christmas cards all around the fireplace . . . put candles in the front windows of the house . . . hang the little angel with spun glass wings on the topmost branch of the Christmas tree. Such memories shaped in me attitudes of love toward the past and all the family that was involved in it.

If we don't have a nearby grandparent to help with the

Christmas traditions, we should take the time and effort to do it ourselves. The special thing that seems too much bother may be just the thing to preserve family importance in the life of our children.

Occasionally children seem to reject doing the old traditional thing, but when we suggest eliminating the tradition, they rise up in loud protest. In an insecure society, kids are motivated to hang onto all the security that tradition affords them. It's part of what they can depend on to be stable and unchanging, the things about which they can say, "Remember, when we were little, how mom would always?. . ."

One woman told me that a traditional holiday activity at her house is the dragging out of the old home movies made when the youngsters were small. Viewing their own early days seems to be extremely precious to the teenagers, especially. It reinforces their security to be reminded of their roots. It's as if the movies say to their subconscious minds, "See? A long time ago, your family was here in love together, and they're still here in love together. This is something you can count on forever."

It's good for teens to have that kind of assurance tucked away in their minds as they go back out into a world that offers rampant insecurity for their day-to-day lives.

Some Christians find themselves rejecting various meaningful holiday celebrations just because sin has gotten into them and marred what used to be good clean fun.

It's not partaking of wickedness or idolatry to let our little children dress up and go around the neighborhood ringing doorbells of friends' homes on Halloween. It's partaking of loving one another. We don't have to succumb to the insidious attack of the enemy to ruin a day of fun and spoil this area of human relationships.

No four-year-old, giggling behind a Mickey Mouse mask

as he rings his next-door neighbor's doorbell, is planning any kind of awful vengeance if no treat is forthcoming when he stammers, "Trick or treat."

The loving neighbor has been counting on having the little kid come, and is all set to drop some favorite cookies and a popcorn ball into the trick-or-treat bag.

Some Christians have become so superspiritual that they can't join in wholehearted observance of Christmas traditions. I say, "Keep the big Christmas dinner, keep the special programs in the church, and let your kid write his letter to Santa Claus." My kids have never "believed" in Santa Claus, but that hasn't kept them from having exciting anticipations about Christmas.

At Sunday school, when Debbie was quite small, someone wanted to hang up a picture of Santa Claus, but another child in the class objected to it. When Debbie came home and told me about it, I didn't take sides, I just asked her how she felt.

"Well, mom," she said, "I told them they might just as well go ahead and put the picture up, because he's not real anyway." It was no big deal, Debbie went on to explain to me, as she shrugged her little shoulders with an air of wordly wisdom.

If children had childhood made precious by the observance of more instead of fewer family traditions, there might be fewer adults visiting psychiatrists in search of something stable for their lives.

We can make lasting relationships in our family and community for them by giving our children opportunities to be part of everything good that is going on. Working together in church and family programs fosters healthy attitudes toward the community, and gives our child a chance to get acquainted with new people and to learn to love them. Every time we encourage wholesome interaction, we make an opportunity for love to grow.

I see three general attitudes among parents whose children are still at home and who are presenting some problems in their struggle for maturity. First, some parents give up the training in self-defeat; they throw all discipline out the window. They stop trying because they feel there's no way they can win.

A second group of parents insist that they are not guilty of any shortcomings in their efforts to bring their child up properly but that he is going bad all on his own.

A third, the healthiest attitude, is found among parents who acknowledge, "Yes, we've made mistakes and we can't undo them. But we'll try to do better now that we know better."

What if we have failed with our kids? We've done the best we could—or we haven't done the best we could. But there's no way to back up and start over, no matter how much we might yearn to do just that. What then? Do we have to be haunted by our failure forever?

No, God has promised to redeem everything we give to Him. And one of the first steps in Christian maturity and in Christian parenthood is to become aware of what God will do and what He won't do. Basically, He will do what we can't do, but He won't do what we can do for ourselves. What we can do for ourselves, He doesn't need to do for us.

When we're wrong, we can admit it. We can confess our own shortcomings to our children, acknowledge that we're human and that we do make mistakes. We can explain to them that we're striving toward the perfection of Christ in us but that we haven't reached it yet. And if we let them see that God is training us day by day, they'll take it in stride and be stronger for knowing it.

A woman told me about a word that had come to her from the Lord, kind of like a prophecy. He had promised her and her family salvation because of her faithfulness to Him. He said that if she would take her hands off her family and release them to Him, and keep continually committing them to Him, He would do in supernatural ways the things her own hands could never do.

God proves that to us, over and over again. We have to keep on committing our children to Him and acknowledge that He is the one who is doing the work in their lives. If we are worried and up-tight about the well-being of our children, we are actually tying God's hands. When we commit them to Him, we let Him do what He wants with them, not what we had in mind. Our own desires for them might not be what His desires are. But when our desire for them is that His desire for them shall be accomplished, then He can go ahead and do exceeding abundantly, above all we could ask or think. At that point, living with our kids will hold for us the kind of joy God planned for us from the beginning.

Appendix

Some Books to Help You with the Sex Education of Your Child:

Andrey, Andrew C., and Schepp, Steven. How Babies Are Made. New York: Time-Life Books, © 1968. (Ages 3-10)

Beck, Lester F. Human Growth: The Story of How Life Begins and Goes On. New York: Harcourt, Brace, and World, © 1949. (Early teens)

Bendick, Jeanne. What Made You You? New York: McGraw-Hill, © 1971.

Buckingham, Jamie. Coming Alive. Plainfield, New Jersey: Logos, © 1970. (Grades 5 and 6)

Buckingham, Jamie. Your New Look. Plainfield, New Jersey: Logos, © 1970. (Junior high age)

Crawford, Kenneth. Growing Up with Sex. Nashville, Tennessee: Broadman Press, © 1973. (Sexuality in Christian Living) (Junior high)

de Schweinitz, Karl. Growing Up: How We Become Alive, Are Born, and Grow. New York: Macmillan, © 1965. (Middle grades)

Edens, David. The Changing Me. Nashville, Tennessee: Broadman Press, © 1973. (Sexuality in Christian Living) (Ages 9-11)

Evans, Eva Knox. The Beginning of Life: How Babies Are Born. London: Crowell-Collier Press, © 1969.

Frey, Marguerite Kurth. I Wonder, I Wonder. St. Louis, Missouri: Concordia Publishing House, © 1967. (Concordia Sex Education series) (Ages 5-9)

Gruenberg, Sidonie Matsner. The Wonderful Story of How You Were Born. Garden City, New York: Doubleday, © 1959. (Middle grades and junior high)

Gruenberg, Benjamin C. and Gruenberg, Sidonie M. The Wonderful Story of You: Your Body—Your Mind—Your Feelings. Garden City, New York: Garden City Books, © 1960. (Middle grades and junior high)

Harty, Robert, and Harty, Annelle. Made to Grow. Nashville, Tennessee: Broadman Press, © 1973. (Sexuality in Christian Living) (Ages 6-8)

Hofstein, Sadie. The Human Story: Facts on Birth, Growth, and Reproduction. New York: Lothrop, Lee and Shepard, © 1967. (Ages 10-14)

Howell, John C. Teaching Your Children About Sex. Nashville, Tennessee: Broadman Press, © 1967. (Sexuality in Christian Living)

Lerrigo, Marion O. A Story About You. New York, Dutton, © 1969. (Grades 4-7)

Lester, Andrew D. Sex Is More Than a Word. Nashville, Tennessee: Broadman Press, © 1973. (Sexuality in Christian Living) (Senior high)

Levine, Milton I. and Seligmann, Jean H. The Wonder of Life. New York: Golden Press, © 1968. (Grades 5-9)

Narramore, Clyde M. Life and Love. Grand Rapids, Michigan: Zondervan, © 1968. (Pre-adolescent)

Narramore, Clyde M. How to Tell Your Children About Sex. Grand Rapids, Michigan: Zondervan, © 1958.

Power, Jules. How Life Begins. New York: Simon & Schuster, © 1968. (Grades 4-9)

Sheffield, Margaret. Where Do Babies Come From? New York: Knopf, © 1972.

Showers, Paul and Showers, Kay Sperry. Before You Were a Baby. New York: Thomas Y. Crowell, © 1968. (Let's Read and Find Out Science Books)

Silverstein, Dr. Alvin, and Silverstein, Virginia B. The Reproductive System: How Living Creatures Multiply. Englewood Cliffs, New Jersey: Prentice-Hall, © 1971.

Strain, Frances Bruce. Being Born. New York: Appleton-Century-Crofts, © 1954.

Taylor, Kenneth N. Almost Twelve; The Story of Sex for Children. Wheaton, Illinois: Tyndale House, © 1968.